OCEANIA
Polynesia, Melanesia, Micronesia

OCEANIA
Polynesia, Melanesia, Micronesia

Charles Paul May

THOMAS NELSON INC.
Nashville • Camden • New York

Johnston Island.

Acknowledgments

The author wishes to express special thanks to John Abernethy, Bruce and Mrs. Allardice, Paul and Mrs. Biggins, Robert A. Carlisle, Elaine S. Cruz, Ralph Eades, Patricia Flynn, R. L. Gaal, James Gilman, Anne Godden, Richard Griffin, Charles W. and Mrs. Harrison, Samuel Heller, Patricia Howarth, Bernie Knowles, Andrew Low, James H. Manke, Gervan McCune, Terry V. McIntyre, George M. Miyachi, Peter and Mrs. Mouka, Patrick Sheahan and family, Ivan Southall and family, and Sifa and Mrs. Tafisi. Among the dozens of other people who helped him, he is grateful particularly to the employees and residents of the Beach House in Nukualofa, the Outrigger in Suva, and Aggie Grey's in Apia.

The author would like to thank the following sources for granting him permission to use their photographs: R. Wenkam, Guam Visitors Bureau; Qantas Airways; French Embassy and Information Division; Office of Territories, U.S. Department of the Interior; U.S. Army; U.S. Navy; U.S. Coast Guard; World Health Organization, United Nations; Food and Agriculture Organization, United Nations; New Zealand Information Service; Tahiti Tourist Board; Public Information Division, Trust Territory of the Pacific Islands; The Metropolitan Museum of Art, Bequest of Samuel A. Lewisohn; and Ewin Galloway. Other photographs by Charles Paul May.

Second Printing

Library of Congress Cataloging in Publication Data

May, Charles Paul.
    Oceania: Polynesia, Melanesia, Micronesia.

    (World neighbors)
    SUMMARY: Discusses the geography, history, politics, culture, and people of the Pacific Islands.
    Bibliography: p.
    1.   Islands of the Pacific—Juvenile literature. [1.   Islands of the Pacific]
I.   Title.
DU17.M39   919   72–13152
ISBN 0–8407–7068–5
ISBN 0–8407–7069–3 (lib. bdg.)

To Kathleen Leerburger and Eleanor Wood
and to Kenneth V. Marr and family

Also by Charles Paul May

Animals of the Far North
Bats
Book of American Birds
Book of Canadian Animals
Book of Insects
Book of Reptiles and Amphibians
Box Turtle Lives in Armor
Central America: Lands Seeking Unity
Chile: Progress on Trial
The Early Indians: Their Natural and Imaginary Worlds
Great Cities of Canada
High-Noon Rocket
James Clerk Maxwell and Electromagnetism
Little Mouse
Michael Faraday and the Electric Dynamo
Peru, Bolivia, Ecuador: The Indian Andes
A Second Book of Canadian Animals
Stranger in the Storm
Veterinarians and Their Patients
When Animals Change Clothes
Women in Aeronautics

Map courtesy of *Encyclopedia International,* published by Grolier Incorporated, New York.

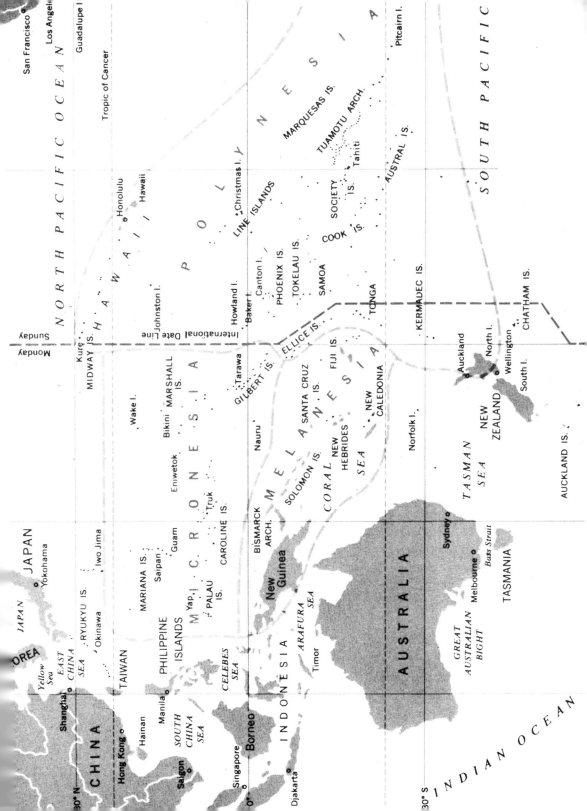

Contents

A taxi driver of Tonga feels he has a special skill that sets him apart.

Small Islands in a Giant Ocean

The islands of the Pacific Ocean stretch south from Alaska to Australia and east from the Philippines to Chile. The equator runs straight from Ecuador on South America's western hump to just south of Singapore on the southeastern tip of mainland Asia, and separates the north and south seas. Only those spots of land south of this imaginary line can truly be called South Pacific islands, but careless usage has allowed many of the islands north of the equator to go by that name as well. It is these islands in the whole area loosely called the South Pacific that are known as Oceania.

Many of the islands lying around the edges of the Pacific, including Japan and the Philippines, are not considered a part of Oceania. Others, such as Hawaii and New Guinea, are part of it, but they receive so much coverage in other books that they will get little mention here. However, a few thousand other islands remain in the vast area of ocean that lies farther south than Japan and north of New Zealand. They can be divided into three main groups.

The Three Areas of Oceania

Roughly, those islands in the central and eastern Pacific make up what is called Polynesia. They include Hawaii, the Samoas, Tonga, the Cook and Society islands, and the Marquesas. The western Pacific islands south of the equator are called Melanesia, and include New Guinea, the

Active Yasur volcano keeps part of Tanna, an island of the New Hebrides group, from being livable, and the World Health Organization has had to help these people.

11

Fijis, the Admiralties, the Solomons, the New Hebrides, and New Caledonia. In the western ocean, most of them north of the equator, are the islands of the Carolines, Gilberts, Marianas, and Marshalls. They form Micronesia.

Polynesia

The word "Polynesia" means "many islands." The name hardly distinguishes the area from Melanesia and Micronesia, for they, too, have hundreds of dots of land. However, great numbers of the Polynesians differ in appearance from the people to the west. In general, they are brown to golden yellow and have Caucasian features—that is, a facial structure similar to that of many white people in Europe. Their dark-brown to black hair is wavy, and they are medium tall.

Melanesia

Melanesians are generally darker and shorter than Polynesians. Like some peoples of Africa, they often have wide, flat noses and somewhat thickened lips. A person's black hair, sometimes referred to as frizzy,

Native musicians of Fiji welcome tourists.

stands out from his head in a kinky ball if allowed to grow long. Yet the name "Melanesia," or "black islands," didn't come from the appearance of the people. Early navigators thought the islands looked black against the horizon.

Micronesia

From a distance, the islands of Micronesia also look dark. Their name means "small islands," again a term suitable for the other regions of Oceania. Micronesians are a mixture of many races, including Polynesian and Melanesian. But anthropologists, scientists who try to classify people, say the Micronesians have more Oriental features than the other two groups. Otherwise, except for their short stature, they probably resemble Polynesians more than they do Melanesians.

The World of Oceania

There is no consistent pattern to life in Oceania. Whatever can be said about the way one man lives there, can often be said of another a thousand miles away from him. At the same time he may be quite different from someone living on the next island, which might be ten miles away or five hundred. Oceania is huge.

Conflicts rage today in this area, as they have in the past. Under the surface of the world's largest body of water—an ocean big enough to swallow all the land on earth—struggles go on constantly. The crown of thorns starfish devours defenseless coral polyps; both man and the triton, a giant snail, hunt the crown of thorns. Volcanoes erupt. Not even the air above the islands knows peace. Some of the worst storms on earth—typhoons—do more damage to Pacific lands than wars have done.

In this great expanse, in the midst of untamed nature, some people are so remote from population centers that they see no outsiders for years; others depend on outsiders for their livelihood.

In a changing world many island people still try to hold on to their age-old customs, and although the money that tourists bring in is attractive to their governments, many would like to keep the tourist himself away. The foreign sightseer is a disruptive presence. The clothes he wears, the wristwatch on his arm, the money in his wallet, all indicate other ways of life, and an islander does not always know whether those ways are better than his own or not.

Scientific and technological advances that will increase agricultural production or make industry more profitable are, of course, welcome in Oceania, but the Pacific islanders have fervently wished for many years that foreign powers would go elsewhere to test their atomic and hydrogen bombs.

Kinky hair indicates that the man making basket for Coke-sipping Australian tourists is a Melanesian.

Straight hair and lack of Oriental features indicate that these marble players are east of the Date Line—in Polynesia.

It has been 450 years since the first white men ventured into Oceania and began dividing it into the regions recognized today and adding to its problems. When the white men came, the Melanesians, Micronesians, and Polynesians had already been on some of the islands for hundreds of years. No one knows for how many hundreds of thousands of years the islands existed with no life, plant or animal, on them at all.

Beginnings

The peoples of the Pacific tell legends to explain how their islands came into being. According to the Polynesians, many spirits existed before the world was made. In one tale, the creator spirit produced a world that was all water. He called on the sea god, Tangaroa (also spelled Taaroa or Tangaloa) to do something about it. Tangaroa had a magic hook. Dropping it into the water, he caught it in some mud and gave an upward heave. Out popped an island. Because the world was huge, he brought more and more specks of land to the surface.

Scientists are noted for puncturing romantic stories, so we can hardly expect them to accept such a legend. They tell us that all of the islands of Oceania resulted from the activities of mammoth volcanoes or of little animals.

Mountains and Little Animals

Mountain-building volcanoes occur under water as well as on land, heaving up ranges that compare with the Rockies and the Himalayas. The peaks that reach above sea level are islands. In Melanesia the islands of New Caledonia are the highest peaks of one mountain range, while the Solomons, the Santa Cruz Islands, and the New Hebrides comprise another group. The Fiji Islands in that area are a separate range. Farther east, in Polynesia, rise the Samoan, Society, Tubuai, and Marquesas islands as high points of yet other volcanic ranges.

Coconuts probably reached Oceania before man did.

At one time many of these islands may have rivaled Hawaii's Mauna Loa, which towers nearly 14,000 feet above the sea, but heavy rains and countless centuries of fierce storms have worn the peaks down. Some are only a few thousand feet above sea level today. Even so, the high point of the Solomons stands more than 10,000 feet above sea level, and the Society Islands have some 8,000-foot peaks.

By contrast, the islands built by little animals are generally quite low, perhaps ten to twenty feet above sea level at high tide. The ones in the Tuamotu Archipelago, south of the Marquesas, have been called the Low, or Dangerous, Islands because they barely rise out of the water and have wrecked many ships. Often these low islands are called atolls, or coral atolls.

Coral is formed by tiny sea creatures known as polyps. Each polyp

Though most rivers in Oceania are short, much rainfall and steep mountains create rushing streams on volcanic islands.

A coral coastline on Tongatapu, where erosion has carved what looks like a camel's head.

has a saclike body with an opening, or mouth, at the top end. The food and water passing into a polyp's mouth contain calcium carbonate, the main component of limestone. The polyp can pass this calcium carbonate through the walls of its body, and combine it with another ingredient that makes it harden. As the calcareous material passes through the body wall, it becomes solid and forms a stonelike cup around the polyp. The animal lives stuck within this pocket, and when it dies, the hard cup remains.

Most polyps live in colonies. Before one animal in a group dies, one or more bumps, or buds, grow from its outer skin. These turn into new polyps, which secrete their calcium carbonate pockets onto the cup already formed by their parent. In this way a colony gradually expands.

19

Some colonies grow less than an inch a year; others grow several inches. Obviously, the reefs and atolls of the Pacific resulted from hundreds of thousands of years of this coral building.

In the nineteenth century, some scientists thought coral extended above the sea when polyps below the top layer pushed others upward. Today researchers say that can't happen, for only the outermost layer of polyps in a group remains alive. Since they are firmly attached and cannot go hunting, the polyps depend on the water in which they live to bring food near them. The most they can do is wave tentacles—tiny armlike growths—and create currents to carry food toward their mouth. They cannot build themselves higher than sea level, for in doing so they would cut themselves off from food and quickly starve.

How then have the coral structures of the Pacific risen into the air?

Polyps generally live in shallow water. Far out at sea, the water is shallow where mountaintops have not quite reached the surface. Once the polyps have produced large colonies along the rim of a volcanic crater, a bit more earth-moving activity within the mountain can shove the coral into the air.

In other cases, polyps have built on the underwater slopes of a volcanic island. After erosion erased the island, the coral remained, to rise above the water when uplifting occurred. Also, when the world was much warmer, the oceans were deeper than they are today. As ice formed at the North and South Poles and in glaciers, the oceans fell a little, leaving coral islands exposed. In a few cases, earthquakes or volcanic activity on the sea floor have been strong enough to raise coral hundreds of feet above sea level.

Colonies of coral-building polyps don't produce solid doughnut-shaped walls, but leave gaps in them. As a colony emerges into the air, waves keep the gaps open, so a coral island has a disconnected outline. Instead of being a solid mass, it will usually be a broken ring or horse-shoe of stony islets separated by channels. Its interior section will be a body of water. For this reason, the name "atoll," meaning land enclosing a lagoon, has been applied to low coral islands.

Volcanic islands of the Pacific grow thick with vegetation.

Soil and Life Arrive in Oceania

Oceania's volcanic islands consist mostly of basaltic, or volcanic, rocks. Neither these rocks nor the stonelike coral of atolls offers soil in which vegetation can grow. Yet the islands of the Pacific carry ferns, bushes, and trees, and even the atolls support palms and some other plants. Their surfaces had to acquire soil somehow. The action of winds, rains, and waves continually works to break up solid masses of hard materials. Over hundreds of years, the rock and coral surfaces broke down under this action until they formed a kind of soil. Storms blowing from Asia or South America carried trees and other plants out to sea. The first of this vegetation to reach Oceania washed up on beaches

Even the commonest orchids of the Pacific are lovely.

and rotted there, adding to the soil. Sea creatures, tossed ashore by waves, also decomposed and enriched the land.

Once a rich enough soil existed, plants that washed ashore with their roots intact gained a foothold and began to grow. Birds from the continents, flying far out to sea, sometimes reached Oceania. Seeds they had swallowed passed through their bodies, sprouted in the soil, and added more vegetation.

Scientists disagree as to which plants existed on the Pacific islands before the arrival of men and which ones came in the canoes of the first navigators. Coconuts sometimes float for hundreds of miles and could have been growing in Oceania before men got there. The breadfruit, shaped like a melon or a cannonball, might also have preceded man. Less important for food but valuable for construction, the pandanus, or screw pine, probably existed in Oceania long before the arrival of human beings. A few types of sandalwood trees may also have grown in the islands before men came. So may have lauans, which produce a wood that resembles and is often called mahogany.

When man began to venture out upon the Pacific, he probably brought with him the taro, a big-leaved plant that has an edible tuber, or underground stem, and scientists feel certain that men brought yams, bananas, and sugarcane for use as food. However, plants that are appreciated primarily for their beauty most likely drifted to the islands. If men did bring them, it must have been after they had time to think of more than mere survival. Among the gorgeous flowers of Oceania are the highly fragrant frangipani and the showy hibiscus and bougainvillea. Pacific islands also produce dozens of varieties of orchids.

Once plants began to grow, animals could find food and survive on the islands and atolls. Riding on the vegetation that floated to the islands would have been flies, moths, butterflies, and other insects or their eggs. Millipedes, centipedes, spiders, and scorpions could survive once they had insects for food.

Sea birds easily reached the islands before men. They included noddies and other terns, boobies, gannets, cormorants, gulls, and petrels. Some land birds—such as parrots, fruit doves, short-eared owls, swifts, and honey eaters—also made their way to Oceania. Sea birds frequently nested in large colonies, as they still do, hundreds of birds sometimes crowding together on a small island. As their droppings piled up year after year, the island became rich in a natural fertilizer known as guano, which contains minerals from the bodies of the fish eaten by the birds. When plowed into the ground, these minerals help plants to thrive, so men mine the guano deposits today for use as fertilizer.

Reptiles and amphibians probably reached many islands long before man. Melanesia boasts the widest assortment, followed by Micronesia. Ocean-swimming crocodiles, which make their homes in both areas, probably arrived by swimming from island to island. Melanesia's iguanas, some of which reach several feet in length, may have arrived in the same way. It is more likely, however, that they drifted to Oceania on floating vegetation, along with smaller reptiles, such as geckos and skinks, and common green frogs, tree frogs, narrow-mouthed frogs, and other amphibians.

Snakes could have reached Oceania by swimming or by rafting on plant materials. Since most snakes eat only every few days, they could have drifted long distances without starving. Otherwise they probably caught frogs or blue-tailed skinks traveling on the same vegetation they occupied. Although many islands are without snakes today, scientists say they could have had some at one time. The Solomons, Fijis, and Samoas contain more snakes than most other regions. Found mostly in Melanesia and Polynesia are the constrictors known as boas. Blind snakes inhabit all three sections of Oceania. Generally less than a foot in length and with scales hardly noticeable to the unaided eye, they look like huge worms. They aren't necessarily blind, but their eyes may be so small as to escape notice. Boas and blind snakes are harmless to man, but in the Fiji Islands lives a viper whose bite can make an adult person sick. Also to be avoided are poisonous sea snakes which make their homes along the coastlines in all three areas of Oceania.

Turtles can be found throughout Micronesia, Melanesia, and Polynesia. Most of them live in the sea and come ashore on the islands only to lay their eggs. But there are also large land turtles, particularly

Some turtles of the Pacific grow to great size.

Fruit-eating bats have served as food for hungry islanders, but these of Tonga can be hunted only by the royal family.

in Melanesia, with backs that seem to be made of leather rather than shell, and vicious snapping turtles that can rip off the toe of an unwary swimmer. They may have swum to islands from the mainland or traveled on large plants.

Mammals had to find other ways of getting to the islands, although some drifted to Oceania aboard rafts of vegetation. Others, like pigs and dogs, and possibly rats and mice, came in the canoes of the early navigators. Of the vast assortment of the world's mammals, only one—the bat—made it to Oceania under its own steam. The only mammals capable of true flight, bats were living in the caves and trees of the islands while men were still confined to the shores of Asia.

Sea creatures abound in all parts of Oceania, and before men arrived, there were even more. Great schools of whales once lived in the region or passed among the islands during migrations to or from breeding

25

Water buffalo, such as this one in the Marianas, have been brought to Oceania in modern times.

grounds or feasting places. Now groups of whales are much smaller, reduced by greedy whalers of the past two hundred years. Rays and sharks still swim through clear waters in search of small fishes as brightly colored as decorations on a Christmas tree, and flying fishes break the surface, spreading their winglike fins to glide away from pursuing dolphins.

Man Ventures upon the Pacific

What brought man to this watery region dotted with tiny spots of land? Probably the early explorers sought what man still seeks—a chance to be free and independent. Some early arrivals may have been blown far off course from the shores of Asia, the Philippines, or Australia, but anthropologists believe that most Oceanic peoples journeyed there intentionally. They probably came from Asia, although the Norwegian scientist Thor Heyerdahl sailed his raft *Kon-Tiki* to Oceania from Peru to prove that people might have come from South America.

More than two thousand years before the birth of Christ, according to many scientists, peaceful peoples lived along the coasts of southeast Asia. From the north, where China now exists, warlike tribes came to trouble them. The peaceful men moved down the Malayan Peninsula and made short trips to the nearest islands of what is now Indonesia. When intruders continued to harass them, they sailed in dugout canoes to islands farther away, such as the Philippines. Being close observers of nature, they had probably seen vegetation floating to their shores when winds blew from the sea or noticed flocks of birds flying out over the water and not returning. So they sailed with a fair expectation of reaching land.

Trade Winds and Ocean Currents

The earliest voyages from the Asian mainland may have been made in small fishing boats. But in time the people developed oceangoing canoes to carry groups of families. Using stone tools, the navigators

Fishermen may have been blown to some parts of Oceania.

27

The outrigger canoe replaced the catamaran as the main boat of Oceania before white men arrived.

hollowed out canoes from tree trunks eighty to a hundred feet long. Then across two canoes they built a platform of coconut-tree planks, which were lashed to each other and to the canoes with ropes of vegetable fibers, usually made of bamboo or rattan. One or two cabins stood on the platform, which also held a fireplace of sand and rocks so the women could cook during trips. This vessel, called a catamaran today, carried a large triangular sail woven of coconut or pandanus leaves.

By day, the sailors took their bearings from the sun, from the behavior of the waves, and from the directions in which birds flew. At night they watched the moon and stars. Even when the skies were overcast, the prevailing winds and water currents still gave some indication of direction. Certain winds above the equator, coming from the north and east and blowing westward, have become known as the northeasterlies, or northeast trade winds. Other winds below the equator, coming from the south and east are called southeasterlies, or the southeast trades. The sailors learned to take them into account. They also learned to expect severe storms between July and October, but sometimes as early as March and as late as November. These tropical cyclones, or typhoons, whirling in a counterclockwise direction north of the equator and in a clockwise direction in the south, might reach speeds of a hundred to two hundred miles an hour.

Besides currents in the air, there were currents in the oceans for the travelers to follow and, sometimes, to fight. In Oceania, the current just north of the equator, the north equatorial countercurrent, generally flows toward the east; the one farther north, the north equatorial current, moves westward. South of the equator, another stream of water, the south equatorial current, moves toward the west. And below this, the south equatorial countercurrent flows east. To sail eastward from the Philippines and Indonesia, the early navigators sailed against the prevailing winds and sometimes against the ocean currents as well.

For long voyages, the early seamen often carried frigate birds on their catamarans. After weeks at sea, especially if supplies began to run short, they released one or more of the birds. A frigate bird circled high into the sky, and if it sighted land, it generally flew in that direction. Following the line of flight, the navigators could proceed to the nearest island.

In Search of New Lands

Voyagers from the Philippines reached Micronesia about fifteen hundred years before the birth of Christ. Melanesia was settled even earlier, perhaps by travelers from Indonesia. The first people to sight Polynesian lands came from Micronesia or Melanesia around 800 B.C.

No one knows for sure why some of the island peoples kept moving farther east. One theory is that the darker-skinned peoples of Melanesia drove the lighter-skinned ones out. It has also been suggested that the lighter peoples suffered more than the dark ones from the diseases of Melanesia, especially malaria. Polynesia has fewer malarial mosquitoes than Melanesia.

The search for food may have driven some people on from one island to another. A woman digs for crabs, which quickly disappear into their holes when anything approaches.

Mongoloid peoples from northern Asia may have pushed some families from Micronesia to Polynesia. The poor soils of coral islands sent others in search of better farming country. It is doubtful that overcrowding played much part in keeping peoples on the move. In any case, dark-skinned peoples remained in Melanesia, and those with lighter coloring moved on eastward. Farther north, many Micronesians remained to intermarry with the Orientals and so acquired some of their characteristics.

Some scientists think Tonga was the first Polynesian island to be discovered soon after Fiji, farther northwest in Melanesia, had been settled. Perhaps so, but many anthropologists think Samoa, which is north of Tonga, became the first major area of settlement in Polynesia, having been reached by light-skinned men and women from either Micronesia or Melanesia. In fact, Tonga, Tahiti, Hawaii, and many other parts of Polynesia may have acquired most of their early settlers from the Samoan Islands.

Voyagers didn't cross the Pacific in a continual flow, of course. When they found islands that suited their purpose, they settled down for long periods. After dozens, perhaps hundreds, of years some of their descendants sailed in search of new lands. Although most islands of Melanesia and Micronesia had probably been visited or sighted by the time Christ was born, it may have been as late as A.D. 1300 before the easternmost islands of Polynesia received inhabitants. By this time, the explorers of Europe had developed ships in which they dared to venture far from shore. Vikings, sailing out on the North Atlantic, had settled on Iceland and Greenland. They had probably reached some part of North America as early as the year 1000. As European seamen became more adventurous, they were certain to reach Oceania.

31

Outsiders Move In

In September 1513, a Spanish adventurer named Vasco Nuñez de Balboa crossed the Isthmus of Panama and discovered an ocean, which he called the South Sea. "Discovered" in this case means that he recorded what he saw with written words. Millions of mainland Asians, Micronesians, Melanesians, Polynesians, and Indians had seen this ocean centuries before Balboa did, but he may have been the first man to suspect it wasn't part of the Atlantic and that the world had more than one great body of water. Naturally, Balboa had no way of knowing that the ocean he faced was twice as big as the Atlantic.

Seven years after Balboa sighted the South Sea, Ferdinand Magellan, a Portuguese commanding ships for Spain, actually sailed into the ocean. He had just passed through an amazingly rough channel, now known as the Strait of Magellan, near the tip of South America. By comparison, the sea seemed wonderfully calm, so he gave it a name that meant peaceful—the Pacific. From then on mapmakers and sailors used both names, South Sea and Pacific, interchangeably, until the nineteenth century, when Pacific finally won out.

The First Europeans Cross the Pacific

Magellan believed the world was round, so, upon reaching the Pacific, he sailed boldly westward. More than a month passed, and the year changed to 1521. Another month went by, and February also slipped

Mosaics on the wall of a modern building in Papeete recall events of the *Bounty* adventure.

away. By this time Magellan and his men knew the huge expanse of water could be unpeaceful. They also knew what it meant to be without food and fresh water. How Magellan missed every island and reef of Polynesia and nearly all those of Micronesia, historians will never know. His men lay about the decks so ill or nearly starved that they could hardly move when the lookout at last hoarsely called out that he saw land.

On March 6, 1521, the Spanish ships reached Guam, in what we now call the Marianas. They are the most northwesterly islands of Micronesia, which means that for about seven thousand miles and more than two months Magellan had been sailing near or among the islands of Oceania.

The Europeans and the people of the Marianas marveled at each other's boats. The Micronesians had war canoes fifteen feet longer than Magellan's flagship, the *Trinidad*, which was only eighty-seven feet long. A war canoe had a long, narrow float out to one side to help keep it

Ships of various sorts are still the main links between many islands.

The royal tomb in the background (in Western Samoa) shows the white man's influence, but old-style pyramid tombs can also be found.

stable in the water. This float, or outrigger, had generally replaced the second canoe of the catamaran by the time Europeans came to the Pacific. The island people had never seen ships without outriggers, and must have wondered what kept Magellan's vessels from rolling over in the water. Nor had they seen guns, crossbows, metal knives, or pails.

Those of Magellan's men who had any strength left went ashore to seek a change from their diet of rats, wormy bread, and ox skins. The naked islanders, curious about the unusual possessions of the white men, began to clutch at everything strange. Perhaps they only wanted to examine the sailors' belongings, but Magellan took them for robbers. He ordered his men to fire. After quickly subduing the astounded islanders, the Europeans loaded their boats with coconuts, fruits, edible roots, and hastily killed pigs. This first meeting between whites and the peoples of Oceania was a portent of the centuries of exploration, settlement, and exploitation that were to follow.

About a week after leaving Guam, Magellan was killed in the Philippines. However, one of his ships managed to finish the trip around the world and finally returned to Spain, where the sailors reported their discovery of the Marianas, which they called the Ladrones, or Thieves' Islands, and amazed Europeans with their tales of the size of the great South Sea.

The Pacific Begins to Yield Its Secrets

The Pacific might have remained at peace if the countries of Europe had been friendly toward one another. Instead, Spain and Portugal began a scramble for new territories and tried to outdo each other in building large empires and gaining treasure. Portugal's Diego da Rocha, sailing northeast from Indonesia in 1526 or 1527, discovered several islands, probably in the western Carolines. No one knows for certain which places he visited there, although he may have reached the island group of Yap. Portugal established no colonies in Oceania following da Rocha's voyage.

A Spaniard, Alvaro de Saavedra, sailed from Mexico, reaching the eastern Caroline Islands on New Year's Day 1528. Claiming them for Spain, he gave his country a basis for later settlements as well as the credit for discovering the Carolines. Saavedra brought changes to Oceania. The Spanish sailors introduced the Micronesian peoples to new animals, such as cattle and goats. Perhaps it's just a joke, but a report says his goats nibbled the grass skirts off the people of Truk in the Carolines. In the way of crops, he brought corn and coffee. Unfortunately, his sailors carried diseases unknown to the islanders and against which they had no natural resistance. Thousands of island people died as a result of influenza, measles, and other ailments.

Portugal soon lost out in the race to claim islands of the Pacific. As early as 1493, Pope Alexander VI had drawn the Line of Demarcation—an imaginary line from north to south in the Atlantic—that gave half the world to Spain for exploration and half to Portugal. At that time most Europeans thought the world was flat. They knew nothing of the

Pacific. After Magellan's sailors proved the world was a globe, the Demarcation Line had to be extended. Spain and Portugal reached an agreement in 1529 that it should fall just east of the Philippines. That left all of Oceania for Spain to investigate.

The Spanish Explorers

The names of many explorers have been lost, and we know almost nothing about some of the others. We do know that Ruy López de Villalobos, sailing for Spain in 1543, discovered the Palau Islands in the Caroline group. He probably came from the Philippines, which lay only five hundred miles away.

Nearly a quarter of a century later, Álvaro de Mendaña de Neyra set out from Peru and, in 1568, reached a group of islands he called the Solomons. He claimed he saw local people wearing gold decorations and was reminded of the wealth of the biblical King Solomon. Perhaps he just wanted the islands to have a rich-sounding name in order

Some people still fish by casting nets, as their ancestors did before outsiders arrived.

to attract settlers. The Solomon Islands are in Melanesia, so Mendaña, like Magellan, had passed through Polynesia without realizing it existed. Mendaña's name for the Solomons attracted few treasure hunters. By the time word of his discovery had reached the Americas and Europe, galleons were carrying the riches of Mexico and Peru to Spain.

Spain's fortunes finally fell in 1588, when Francis Drake's English fleet destroyed its armada, which was supposed to be invincible. With dozens of ships lost and thousands of men dead, Spain never recovered its mastery of the seas.

Nevertheless, Mendaña had made plans to establish Spanish settlements in the Pacific. By 1595, a quarter of a century after his first voyage, he gathered together a group of colonists willing to settle in his Solomon Islands and again sailed from South America. Now, for the first time, an explorer found a major part of Polynesia in the way. Mendaña

Remote villages show little—if any—Spanish, Dutch, or other influence.

discovered one of the easternmost groups of Oceania, which he named the Islas Marquesas de Don Hurtado Garcia de Mendoza y Cañete, in honor of the wife of the viceroy of Peru, who had helped finance his voyage. The islands are known today only as the Marquesas.

Mendaña sailed on and discovered the Santa Cruz Islands. Thinking they were part of the Solomons, he established his colony there, but it was almost entirely wiped out by hostile natives, malaria, hunger, and dissent. Mendaña died, and his Portuguese pilot, Pedro Fernandes de Queirós, sailed on to the Philippines with the survivors.

Queirós, however, was a strange man, filled with missionary zeal. Eventually he commanded an expedition of his own. Carrying settlers, he set out from Peru in 1605 to find the Solomons and establish another colony. Not knowing Mendaña had gone too far south, he went even farther. That put him below the Marquesas, and there he discovered some of the Tuamotu and Society islands. When he reached Melanesia in 1606, he made his landfall in the New Hebrides.

Queirós put his settlers ashore on an island and helped them start a colony called New Jerusalem. Then one night Queirós himself mysteriously sailed away without a word, leaving his second in command to cope with the colonists.

The Coming of the Missionaries

During the early years of the seventeenth century, Spain began to shift her attention away from the Pacific somewhat as wars with the British and the Dutch kept her occupied closer to home. When she did renew her activities in the South Pacific, she no longer expected to find great fortunes, but showed concern for colonizing and spreading Christianity.

Mariana of Austria, widow of Spain's Philip IV, sent Jesuit missionaries to Oceania in 1667. Settling in northwestern Micronesia, they renamed Magellan's Ladrones the Marianas in the queen's honor.

Nearly twenty years later, Francisco Lazeano followed these Jesuits. He declared Spanish rule over most of the islands of Micronesia and named them the Carolines after Carlos (Charles) II, who, in 1665, had become king of Spain at the age of four.

At first most Oceanic peoples peacefully shared their islands with Europeans, but in time they began to realize that a whole new way of life might replace their own. The missionaries tried to make them wear clothes, give up sleeping in large family groups in one-room huts, and stop doing their body-wiggling dances. With their freedom hampered, the people soon lost interest in Christianity and tried to return to their old customs. The missionaries then introduced force. Some of them sincerely believed that a man was the same as dead if he wasn't a Christian, and they felt they were doing him a favor if they killed him while trying to convert him. Native resistance with weapons of stone and bone was useless against European firearms. In addition, the people had been weakened and their numbers reduced by the diseases of the white man, so rebellions ended in disaster. By the end of the 1600's, only a few thousand people remained in the Carolines, where 20,000 to 30,000 had once lived peacefully. By the 1800's, Spain considered most of Micronesia to belong to her.

The Dutch East India Company and Its Rivals

In the 1500's Spain controlled the provinces north of France called the Netherlands. Toward the end of that century, however, seven of the regions, which included Holland as their chief member, agreed on a union in order to gain strength. Although they remained tied to Spain during the first half of the 1600's, the United Provinces could accomplish feats together that they had been unable to do individually. Among other things, they built ships, and with them they attacked Spanish vessels on the high seas. In time Dutch sails began to appear among the islands of Oceania.

The Dutch government granted a monopoly to the Dutch East India Company, chartered in 1602, on all trade east of Africa and west of the Americas. Through this company, the Dutch controlled the trade in

Malaya, Ceylon, and Indonesia, including the Moluccas, or Spice Islands.

Willem Corneliszoon Schouten had sailed the Indian Ocean in the service of the Dutch East India Company. Eventually he formed his own organization with the merchant Jacob Le Maire, and in 1615 they sought a new route to the spices of Asia. Schouten and Le Maire may have been the first Europeans to sail around Cape Horn on the southern tip of South America instead of through the Strait of Magellan, and they were the ones to give the cape its name—after Schouten's birthplace, Hoorn. They at last reached Polynesia and Melanesia and discovered a number of islands, but trouble had followed them. One of their ships was accidentally burned, and in Indonesia the other was confiscated by the powerful Dutch East India Company, which refused to believe they had found a new route to the Pacific.

The next outstanding Dutch sea captain to make important discoveries in Oceania was Abel Janszoon Tasman. In the service of the Dutch East India Company in the 1640's, he circumnavigated Australia and discovered Tasmania, which he named Van Diemen's Land, and New Zealand. He then sailed north into Polynesia and Melanesia, discovering parts of Tonga and the Fiji Islands.

The Dutch won their independence from Spain through the Treaty of Westphalia in 1648, and began to build a united Kingdom of the Netherlands at home, which left them less time and money for exploration. In the next century Jakob Roggeveen pretty well brought the Dutch Pacific explorations to an end with his 1722 voyage. Like the excursion of Schouten and Le Maire, it was independent of the Dutch East India Company. Roggeveen discovered Easter Island, far west of Chile, and was the first European to see the strange monolithic stone heads that stand there. He named the island after the day on which it was discovered. Traveling north and west, he sighted the Tuamotu Archipelago and, almost straight west of that, discovered the Samoan Islands. In Java, Roggeveen, too, had his ships seized by the Dutch East India Company.

The British and French Arrive

In the eighteenth century British and French voyages to the Pacific increased. Many Englishmen invested in South Pacific ventures, even when they couldn't afford to, and lost a lot of money. After the South Sea Bubble, as it came to be called, had burst, the British government put Oceanic investments on a sounder basis. The bubble affected Britain far more than it did the South Pacific.

Some of the early British expeditions, such as that of George Anson in 1740–1744, attacked Spanish ships in Oceania, but later voyages were primarily scientific. In 1765, Commodore John Byron, grandfather of Lord Byron, the poet, sailed through Polynesia on a geographical survey for the government. Because he frequently ran into trouble, including being shipwrecked, he earned the nickname "Foulweather Jack." Following him two years later, Samuel Wallis discovered two islands in the Marshalls and some in the Society Islands, including Tahiti. He may also have been the first European to sight Wallis Island (named for him) and Futuna islands, west of Samoa.

A bust at the waterfront in Papeete, Tahiti, honors Bougainville.

42

Captain Cook left a marker near the spot where he observed the transit of Venus.

In Tahiti, Wallis and his seamen were the first but not the last Europeans to be beguiled by the climate and the people, and they remained there for some time. They introduced the islanders to nails, but since they could spare only a small number of them, the island women began to offer their favors to seamen for more. According to some stories, the sailors soon started stealing the spikes that held the ships together. Wallis wisely set sail before his vessels fell apart.

In 1768, Captain Louis Antoine de Bougainville, for whom the well-known tropical flower is named, took possession of the Society Islands in the name of France. Bougainville was one of the first captains to treat the islanders with respect. He became popular with the people of Tahiti, which undoubtedly helped France in a later conflict with Britain over the Society Islands. He also introduced turkeys and may have brought wheat to the South Pacific, although the tropics do not provide a good climate for this grain. Besides visiting the Society Islands, Bougainville sailed to the Samoas and New Hebrides. In the

43

Solomons, he discovered the largest island, which now bears his name.

Captain James Cook, in a 1768–1771 voyage that included the exploration of New Zealand and the east coast of Australia, also came to Tahiti. Cook, who was seeking a good place from which to observe a transit of Venus, named the group the Society Islands after the organization backing his voyage—London's Royal Society for Improving Natural Knowledge. During a later voyage, Cook discovered New Caledonia. One group of low atolls he named the Gilberts after his captain, Thomas Gilbert, who was to return nearly twenty years later with an expedition of his own. The Cook Islands, which he discovered in 1773, are, of course, named for Cook himself.

In addition to being the Pacific's greatest explorer, Cook deserves credit for taking more interest in the people than in their lands. From his observations, he called attention to the fact that the people of Oceania were not all alike. For instance, he noted that there was a difference between the people of Polynesia and those of Melanesia. He had left a considerable record of his voyages and observations by the time the people of the Sandwich Islands (Hawaii), which he had discovered, killed him in 1779 during a dispute over a boat.

In 1785, Jean François de Galaup, Comte de La Pérouse, left France on a scientific expedition that he hoped would rival Cook's accomplishments. La Pérouse explored such places as Easter Island, the Sandwich Islands, the Marianas, and Samoa, and kept journals describing the people and sights he saw. Leaving the journals in Australia to be sent to France, he sailed from Botany Bay in 1788 toward New Caledonia and Santa Cruz and was never seen again. La Pérouse's fate is one of the mysteries of the sea (he may have been eaten by cannibals), but the journals he left behind have become classics of Pacific-exploration literature.

Breadfruit and Mutineers

Serving under Captain Cook during one of his Pacific voyages had been a sailing master named William Bligh. This highly capable but extremely strict man returned in 1788, commanding an expedition to collect breadfruit plants in Tahiti for transplanting to islands in the Caribbean. By the time his ship, the *Bounty,* had been loaded with seedlings, many of his men loathed him and looked on the island as a paradise. On April 28, 1789, about three weeks after the *Bounty* left Tahiti, a mutiny broke out, with Bligh's master's mate, Fletcher Christian, taking command of the rebels. The mutineers set Captain Bligh and eighteen of his supporters adrift in an open boat barely large enough to hold them.

The nearest known land proved to be Tofua, in the Tonga Islands, but when Bligh and his companions reached it, they were met by hostile inhabitants. One of the men was killed before the rest shoved the boat away from the shore and paddled to safety.

Sailing west, Bligh next sighted the Fiji Islands, which for a time went by the name of the Bligh Islands. Here canoes set out to meet them, but the people looked so unfriendly that Bligh's men rowed madly to stay ahead of them. Bligh assumed they had escaped the stew pot, for Fiji Islanders were known to be cannibals.

Equipped only with a compass, a quadrant, and a pocket watch, Bligh decided to sail 3,600 nautical miles, or more than 4,000 land miles, to friendly Timor, an island of the Indonesian group claimed by both Portugal and Holland. Along the way, he sighted twenty-three islands whose positions he recorded with great accuracy. After a month, the men were suffering so much from exposure, hunger, and thirst that they no longer had the strength to row. However, the boat's one sail kept the small craft voyaging in the right direction. After forty-one days, they reached Timor, with only one man lost, the one killed on Tofua.

Christian, after setting Bligh's twenty-three-foot boat adrift, took the *Bounty* back to Tahiti. For a brief period the mutineers remained there, enjoying life, but Christian knew an investigation would be made. He, eight of his followers, and eighteen Tahitians sailed the *Bounty* to Pitcairn. This deserted island had been discovered in 1767 by the British captain Philip Carteret and was named for his sailor, Robert Pitcairn, who first sighted it. It had no place for anchoring a ship, which led

Christian to believe British officials would pass it by when searching for the mutineers. After landing their supplies, the mutineers grounded and burned the ship to remove any trace of it.

For a couple of years life on Pitcairn seemed idyllic, but in time the men started fighting over the Tahitian women. When an American whaling vessel discovered the island's secret in 1808, all the *Bounty's* men but one had died or been killed.

Some of the *Bounty*'s men who had remained in the Society Islands fell into the hands of British officials. Three were hanged. But their testimony pointed up the barbaric conditions that existed on many ships making long voyages. Eventually new regulations eased the lives of sail-

White men built lighthouses, such as this century-old landmark, for their own good rather than to aid the local people.

ing men. Bligh himself went back to Tahiti, loaded a vessel with bread-fruit plants, and took them to the Caribbean, but they failed to grow as well or produce as much food there as the British had hoped.

Whales and Pirates

In Oceania, the sixteenth century belonged to the Spanish, the seventeenth century to the Dutch, and the eighteenth century to the British and French. In the nineteenth century, all of them, except the Dutch, continued to be active in the Pacific, with Americans, Russians, and Germans playing an increasingly larger part in the exploration and exploitation of the area. No longer concerned with bringing new spots of land to the world's attention, the seamen now came in search of whales, slaves, bird droppings, and copra. They discovered new islands, but usually by accident while seeking something else. Settlers came, too, and a new era of missionary activity began, bringing with it evil as well as good. But the whalers probably introduced the local people to human nature at its worst.

Whaling reached the Pacific in the 1790's, with American ships setting out from such New England ports as Nantucket and New Bedford. Whale oil could be burned in lamps and made into other useful products, so Britain gave the United States strong competition for a quarter of a century, although France sent only small numbers of ships from time to time. During the War of 1812, American seamen doubled as whalers and privateers, and British vessels stood in danger of being captured or sunk. By the end of the war, United States ships reigned supreme in the Pacific whaling grounds.

Since a whaling vessel stayed at sea until its barrels were filled with oil, voyages sometimes lasted for two or three years. Many men hated to sign up for such long periods, and the better sailors shipped out on other vessels making shorter runs whenever they could. This often left the troublemakers to make up the crews of whaling ships, so the Pacific islanders saw some mighty disorderly and dishonest American and British seamen.

The sailors introduced the local people to rum, started fights, kidnapped women, and stole whatever took their fancy. If an islander tried to get his property back, he probably received a beating. Yet if he stole something from the sailors, he was hunted down and whipped until nearly senseless.

Fearing that they could never find justice in the white man's world, groups of islanders took to piracy to get even. They could always find white leaders if they wanted them, for many criminals had escaped to Oceania, and sailors who had deserted their ships in the South Pacific sometimes welcomed a chance to raid European and American vessels and settlements.

Probably Oceania's best-known and most popular pirate was the British seaman "Bully" Hayes. At sea he looted and if necessary killed to enrich himself. Ashore, however, he would be so charming and generous that many people liked him. He also knew villages where the people would hide him if he needed to stay out of sight for a time. When piracy failed to bring a large enough return, Hayes started dealing in "blackbirds."

The Foul Trade of Blackbirding

Blackbirding, at least in theory, is not quite the same as slave trading. The captive man is rented rather than sold to a master and, supposedly, after a period of servitude gets to go home. Of course, slave trading, as well as blackbirding, went on in the Pacific, and many captives never regained their freedom.

As sugarcane farming increased in Australia, laborers were needed to work in the fields. Many blackbirders took their captives there, although some took islanders to South America for work in mines. Captains filled their ships with human cargo by buying captives after two tribes had been at war. They also promised island men good wages to go abroad to work and took them prisoner after tricking them onto their ships.

The people on the islands of Melanesia, especially Fiji, New Caledonia, the New Hebrides, and the Solomons, suffered most during the period of blackbirding. The easygoing Polynesians refused to be driven to work, and most of Micronesia lay too far away from the Australian plantations to make voyages there as profitable as those to nearby Melanesia.

Wherever they were taken, the Melanesian laborers usually found poor living conditions. Large groups of them slept in small huts, some of which offered little protection from storms. Yet these men fared better than the ones herded together in tightly built wooden shacks, for they became victims of tuberculosis as they coughed or sneezed in one another's faces and breathed the same air over and over. Others encountered smallpox for the first time and succumbed to it. Many plantation owners made no attempt to provide medical care for the workers. On the farms where they did, the "doctor" often turned out to be such a drunkard or so incompetent that the patients refused to see him. On most plantations, fifty to a hundred men out of every thousand died, while in the worst places three quarters of them failed to survive.

Whatever social life the blackbirds had they generally provided for themselves. They sang and told stories to pass the time when not working, but they often worked so hard that they wanted only to eat and sleep if given the chance. A few landowners, trying to be kind-hearted, had women brought from the islands to live with the men, but that generally proved unsatisfactory for all concerned because the men fought over the women, for whom there was no decent housing or medical care.

After his period of servitude ended, a man supposedly was permitted to go back to his island. Usually, no record of where he had been captured existed, and if he failed to explain where he had come from, he might be dumped ashore almost anywhere. Many men then found themselves among strange tribes, who treated them as outcasts. Those who did reach their home villages often found it difficult to return to the old way of life. Others returned safely to find themselves hailed as heroes. Their stories excited wonder among relatives who had never traveled, and the women looked upon them as romantic adventurers.

As more and more missionaries entered the South Pacific, numbers of them objected to the inhuman way the blackbirders treated the people. Unable to frighten the traders with threats of God's wrath, these missionaries called on the governments of the countries from which they had come to end the trade in human beings. Finally, after the mid-1800's, both the British and the French sent officials to investigate.

The first investigators accomplished little. Many of the European settlers distrusted officials from the old country and would tell them nothing. When the investigators went to people in the villages, they found men and women too frightened by what the blackbirders might do later to tell their side of the story.

Made bold by the failure of the early investigations, the blackbirders became more daring. As a result, some islanders began to fight back and launched surprise attacks on European settlements, killing everyone they could. This brought new investigators to Oceania, and a number of sea captains were caught and ordered to stand trial in Australia. Unfortunately Australia lacked laws at that time to deal with the situation, and some judges felt it wasn't their problem anyway. Most blackbirders regained their freedom and returned to their inhuman practices.

In the late 1870's, the people of New Caledonia rebelled in great numbers. Instead of making raids here and there as other islanders were doing, they kept up a sustained resistance and slaughtered foreigners with terrifying savagery. Word of the situation spread around the world, and many governments brought pressure to bear on the British and French to stop the blackbirding trade. In the next decade both countries actively worked to end slaving, and it gradually died away. But it wasn't until the first years of the twentieth century that traffic in Pacific island peoples was outlawed entirely.

Maneuvering for Control of the Pacific

Because of the blackbirders and the men who tried to halt their activities, several island groups of Oceania had become official colonies rather than business outposts of European powers. The French sent

Missionaries introduced schools as well as churches, using one building to house both, as is still sometimes done.

soldiers to the interior of some New Hebrides islands to punish raiders who had fled from the coast. Australia had always looked on this group as being hers, and she feared France intended to take control. Pressure from Australia and Britain forced the French to withdraw and led to a joint French-British Naval Commission to keep the peace. This set the background for joint rule, and today the New Hebrides are still under a British-French condominium.

In other areas, the efforts of missionaries determined the fates of island groups. Catholic missionaries from France had arrived in New Caledonia as early as 1843. In a few years they faced opposition from British seamen and traders, but instead of withdrawing, the Catholics began to promote France as well as Christianity. This activity disturbed New Zealand, within whose jurisdiction Great Britain had placed New

51

Caledonia, but neither English-speaking country made sufficient effort to drive the French out. The French sent settlers in the 1850's and provided troops to help establish a military government.

The same might have happened in the Solomons, except for disease. The Catholic missionaries there became so weakened with malaria that they left. The British, who also suffered from tropical diseases, of course, hardly rushed in to fill the gap. They continued to occupy some settlements, however.

In Polynesia, Protestants of the London Missionary Society and Catholics from France showed less than Christian behavior at times. When the Catholic missionaries came to Tahiti in the 1800's, the Protestants had already been working there since 1797, and they exercised firm control over the local kings of the Pomaré dynasty. The arrival of a French fleet, supposedly to protect Catholics in Polynesia, caused the British representative in the Society Islands to sail to London for help from the Royal Navy. While he was absent, the French declared themselves protectors of Tahiti and its associated islands. Apparently the British didn't consider the area worth struggling over.

The monarch of Tahiti, Queen Pomaré, never fully acknowledged French rule, but after she died in 1877, her son, Pomaré V, showed less concern for his country and his people. He soon gave the French full say in governing Tahiti because they promised him a yearly income that made it possible for him to stay drunk all the time. With Tahiti and nearby islands fully under her control, France increased her influence on other island groups in Polynesia, mainly the Marquesas, Tubuais, Gambiers, and the Tuamotu Archipelago.

In the 1860's, German merchants realized the value of copra, the dried coconut meat that is used in making soaps, cooking oils, perfumes, and the like. The Germans sent seamen and settlers to build a copra industry in the South Pacific. During that time they also discovered that many islands lay under masses of guano. As rapidly as possible, Germany started winning a foothold in Oceania.

As the whaling industry fell off because of fewer whales and because

As buying and selling replaced the old system of barter, markets sprang up and are still common today, like this one in the Fiji Islands.

gas lighting had begun to replace oil lamps since 1860, Americans, too, took more interest in establishing copra bases and seeking guano islands. They also did some religious proselytizing, but not as much as they were to do in the twentieth century.

The Germans, on the other hand, showed little missionary zeal. They wanted islands primarily for trade purposes. Although New Zealand and British settlers lived in the Samoas and the Solomons, German merchants migrated in a stream to those groups. New Zealand became alarmed and prodded Britain to object, but for many years the British showed little concern. In time, the Germans decided they would be stronger if they had complete say in one area rather than partial control in two. They agreed to withdraw from some of the Solomons if Britain and New Zealand gave up their interests in the western Samoas. Eventually the western Samoas became a German colony, while the Solomons remained partly German and partly British. The German masters in Samoa proved harsh, yet they did introduce cocoa, vanilla, and coffee in order to cut down the people's dependence on copra, and the Samoas prospered.

As Germany increased her control over western Samoa, chiefs in the eastern islands asked the United States to take possession there. At first America refused, but President Ulysses S. Grant had heard that the natural harbor of Pago Pago, in the eastern Samoas, was particularly fine and felt it could be useful for military purposes. As a result, the United States established a coaling station at Pago Pago, on Tutuila Island, in 1872. When the Germans took full control of the two largest islands of western Samoa in 1899, the United States did the same in the eastern islands, annexing them as an American territory in 1900. The United States Navy provided the first government.

Spain, having paid only occasional interest to the islands she claimed in Oceania, grew worried as German power increased. In 1875, she announced that all traders in Micronesia must obtain permits from the Spanish government in the Philippines. Most outsiders refused to do this. In such a vast area, Spanish ships could hardly track down and force sea captains to accept their demands. After a decade, Spain made little further effort to patrol Micronesia. That gave German traders enough courage to build a trading center on Yap, in the Carolines, and even fly the German flag there.

Angered, Spain prepared for war. Pope Leo XIII acted as arbitrator in the dispute. He declared that Spain owned the islands but had no right to require trading or fishing permits. Emboldened by this decision, Germany built up her strength on one island after another.

As islands came under stable governments, Oceania, toward the end of the nineteenth century, witnessed an increase in law and order, and

Early visitors to Oceania lived in local-style dwellings, but foreigners who settled down soon introduced European-type houses.

the next great upheaval affecting the area really occurred halfway around the world.

The Spanish-American War

The United States had long objected to Spanish control of Cuba, mostly for selfish reasons. After the Cubans revolted against Spain in 1895, many of them sought safety in the eastern and southern United States. They sent arms and other assistance to the island and encouraged the United States to help Cuba. Certain American newspapers printed stories of Spanish brutality and stirred up a spirit of war.

When an American vessel, the U.S.S. *Maine,* blew up in Havana Harbor, the Americans blamed the Spanish. Two months later the United States Congress resolved to recognize Cuban independence, to demand that Spain withdraw her troops, and to authorize President William McKinley to send soldiers if the Spanish failed to withdraw. Spain took this as a declaration of war. Considering that she had no intention of withdrawing her troops, it was.

During the Spanish-American War, which lasted from April to August 1898, American forces captured the strategically important Pacific island of Guam, at the southern end of the Marianas group, and has continued to hold it ever since. After the war Spain also surrendered the Philippines to the United States, as well as three small islands west of Hawaii. Discovered by Captain William Wake in 1796, they include the islands of Wake, Wilkes, and Peale. Control over all these islands, not to mention Hawaii, which became a United States territory in 1900, greatly increased American influence in the Pacific.

Germany took advantage of the war to strengthen her control over much of Micronesia and, after peace came, bought the Marianas from Spain.

A period of relative quiet followed, but another war, far away from the Pacific, was already in the making, and it would change the balance of power in Oceania considerably.

The World at War

Germany kept warships in Micronesia and the Samoas to discourage any foreign power that might want to add an island to its territory. The Japanese, especially, resented the German occupation of Micronesia, for their islands were becoming overcrowded, and the people needed new farmland. Even before the twentieth century, the Japanese had started to move south, and by 1875 they had forced the Chinese out of Okinawa and the other Ryukyu Islands, which are situated between Taiwan (Formosa) and Japan.

The Bonin and the Volcano Islands lay between Japan and the Marianas. Japan had claimed the Bonins in 1861, although Britain had settlers there, and incorporated them into the Japanese Empire in 1876, confident that Britain wouldn't fight to keep them. It was then an easy step on south to the three Volcano Islands, of which Iwo Jima is one.

The Ryukyus, Bonins, and Volcanos lie outside Micronesia, of course, but they put Japan in a position to move quickly into that area when the chance arose.

The First World War Hits Oceania

The islands of Oceania had been part of the struggle for territory and importance among the most nationalistic countries of Europe in the nineteenth and early twentieth century. When World War I broke out, most of the action took place in Europe and on the Atlantic, but Japan was alert to changes that might favor her in the Pacific.

American troops wade ashore at Guadalcanal.

German naval vessels in the Pacific often anchored in these waters facing Apia, Western Samoa, until most of the ships were called to the Atlantic.

Germany had to call some of her warships to the Atlantic and the North Sea, and she kept only a small fleet, commanded by Admiral Graf von Spee, in the western Pacific to sink British and French merchant vessels there. Almost immediately Japan moved into the Marianas, and the German businessmen there fled.

Britain had the European war to worry about and made no objections to Japan's occupation of the Marianas. Besides, Britain and Japan had signed a treaty in 1902 that said they would not side against each other or help one another's enemies in a conflict, so Britain did not look upon Japan as a threat. The United States felt more threatened from the Atlantic than the Pacific, so she paid little attention, too, except to hang on to Guam.

Taking advantage of the situation, Japan began to occupy the rest of Micronesia. Australia, partly because she was alarmed at Japanese activity and partly to aid Britain, moved north into Melanesia, taking control of German areas in New Guinea and the Solomons. New Zealand had been annoyed over the loss of western Samoa to Germany; she now extended her influence north and landed troops in western Samoa in 1914. Meeting no resistance, she took control there.

The Germans had looked upon the island peoples with indifference or regarded them as servants, making little effort to get to know or understand them. New Zealanders and Australians treated them better. They allowed islanders to go wherever they pleased and to seek jobs for what was considered reasonable wages, and for a brief period the new occupiers proved popular. Unfortunately, they tried to impose too much of their own way of life on the islanders and eventually made some enemies.

Nevertheless, islanders under the New Zealanders and Australians were lucky compared to those under Japan in Micronesia. In the Marianas the Japanese drove the people off the land and turned the islands into a major sugar-producing area. From the Marianas, they moved into the Carolines, Palaus, and Marshalls and tried to force the islanders to work as unpaid or poorly paid laborers. The people resisted, but the Japanese soon quelled them. Many escaped to the jungles or mountains and lived off fruits, bats, and whatever else they could find. The overlords then brought forced labor from the Ryukyus and Korea. Because of this practice, Micronesia's population of 150,000 was nearly half Asiatic by the time of the Second World War.

In the early months of World War I, German submarines and surface vessels caused considerable damage to British and French shipping in the Atlantic. Gradually, however, the Royal Navy developed into an effective force, and Admiral Spee, ordered to the Atlantic, steamed eastward from Micronesia. A few old British vessels sent to intercept him lacked his firepower, and he sank them.

Reaching the South Atlantic, Spee's fleet met with success at first, but better British ships arrived and sank his two heavy cruisers and two of his light cruisers. Spee himself went down with his ship. That left one ship, the *Dresden,* to flee back to the Pacific. Three months later, in March 1915, the British sank it near the Chilean island of Juan Fernández. Spee had sent one other cruiser, the *Emden,* to attack Allied shipping in the Indian Ocean. At first it, too, had considerable success, but an Australian warship ended its career.

With Germany's oceanic fleet destroyed, Japan entered the war on the side of the Allies in August 1915. She drove the Germans from territory they occupied in China, thus making sure that her Micronesian holdings would be safe from a surprise attack by them. Entering the war also increased her chances of keeping the islands when peace came.

Another German naval officer, Felix Graf von Luckner, later came to the Pacific as a raider. His *Seeadler,* disguised as a neutral vessel, escaped British warships but was defeated by the Pacific when a strong tidal wave drove it aground in the Society Islands. Escaping in one of its lifeboats, Luckner, who became known as the Sea Devil, sailed to the Cook Islands. Soon he went on to the Fijis where, in September 1918, British officials recognized and captured him.

Before the end of the war, Japan strengthened her diplomatic ties with

French servicemen on leave in a French Polynesian town.

Britain and signed a secret agreement that ensured her British support in her claim to Micronesian islands north of the equator. On her side, Japan agreed to recognize British Empire claims to Melanesian islands south of the equator.

To cement her position, Japan's diplomats also signed secret agreements with the United States, France, and Russia. At the peace talks in France after the war, Japan used these secret treaties to demand what she wanted in the Pacific. In time, the League of Nations gave her a mandate, which is a commission to establish a government, over the Micronesian islands north of the equator.

Other mandates in Oceania gave New Zealand control over western Samoa and Australia control over the eastern part of New Guinea and Nauru in the central Pacific. The mandatories, as the governing powers were called, could not build military bases in the mandated territories. Instead, they had an obligation to set up systems of government and to educate the islanders so that they could take over their own governments eventually and form independent countries. Western Samoa felt it could govern itself already, but its angry complaints accomplished little. New Zealand proceeded to form the government and to help write laws. The Samoans gradually organized a political party, and by the time World War II began, they had gained some degree of self-rule.

The Between-War Period

As secretly as possible, Japan built military bases in Micronesia. She also tried to undermine United States control of the islands of Guam and Wake. Guam's position, particularly, frustrated Japan. She found it difficult to move in secret as long as the United States had such a convenient lookout point. Nevertheless, Truk and Ponape, in the central Carolines, became major Japanese bases.

In the 1930's, some members of the League of Nations began criticizing Japanese policies in Oceania and continental Asia. By this time Japan felt strong enough to defy the League and the United States. In 1934 she said she would no longer adhere to a treaty—signed in

A signal light along the coast of Howland honors Amelia Earhart, who failed to reach the island.

Washington, D. C., in 1922—that kept her naval power below that of the United States. A year later Japan withdrew from the League of Nations.

During the 1930's, the airplane began to link East and West as ocean-going vessels had never done. In 1928, Australia's Charles Kingsford-Smith, with three companions, flew from California to Australia. Flights from San Francisco to the Philippines the following year further proved that transpacific air travel was feasible. The pace of life in the Pacific grew livelier. Many of Oceania's islands became regular stopping places, first for seaplanes and later for wheeled aircraft. In 1937, Pan American Airways started commercial service across the Pacific, a step toward opening Oceania to tourists who never had time to visit the region by ship.

In Micronesia, Japan discouraged vacationers and even pilots in need of emergency landing places. Rumors still persist that the famous woman aviator Amelia Earhart, lost in Oceania in 1937, had a secret mission to observe Japanese activities from the air. But that seems unlikely. She and her copilot were last seen alive in New Guinea. Their next stop, Howland Island, lay south and east of the Carolines, and to detour over Japanese-held islands would probably have used up too much fuel. Some people say Miss Earhart really intended to fly to Guam, almost straight north of New Guinea. But we know she didn't head toward Guam, because a United States ship, standing by at Howland to guide her with its radio, picked up her voice. Her radio could reach only about five hundred miles, and Howland lies farther than that from the nearest of the Carolines. So she must have been trying to get to Howland. There is no reason to believe that she was in Oceania for any other purpose than to cross it in order to become the first woman to fly around the world.

World War II Begins

After the outbreak of World War II in 1939, Japan became even more aggressive. She tricked Britain and the United States into believing that her first direct move against the Allies would be at Singapore or in Indonesia. Instead, on December 7 (December 8 west of the International Date Line), 1941, she bombed Pearl Harbor, Hawaii, and shelled Midway Island. The next day, Japanese bombers struck Wake. By the twelfth Japan's forces controlled Guam, but five hundred American Marines prevented them from taking Wake until the twenty-third.

After capturing Britain's Gilbert and Ellice Island colony in 1941–1942, Japan occupied all of Micronesia. That finally gave her territory below the equator, because part of the Gilberts and all of the Ellices lie south of that line. It also put Japan on the edge of Polynesia, where the Phoenix Islands, the islands of Baker and Howland, and the northernmost Line Islands lay before her like steppingstones to Hawaii.

The United States quickly built emergency air bases on Kingman Reef and Palmyra Island, members of the Line Islands that were closest to the Hawaiian group. The British gave the United States permission to build bases or to use those being built in other parts of the Line Islands and in the Phoenix Islands.

Japan wanted to cut supply lines between the United States and Australia, but to do that she had to capture Melanesia and parts of Polynesia. In 1942, she took the Solomons and invaded New Guinea, but in the latter she met strong opposition from Australian and American troops.

Japan never gained complete control of New Guinea, and trying to hold on there and in the Solomons kept her from moving south to New Caledonia or southeast to the New Hebrides and Fiji. As a result, New Zealand and the United States used Fiji, New Caledonia, and the New Hebrides as military bases.

The Allies Resist

In 1942, United States intelligence officers broke a secret code used by Japan, and learned that in May the Japanese planned to move a fleet of ships from the Solomons across the Coral Sea to attack Port Moresby, the Allied stronghold in southeastern New Guinea. Aircraft carriers of both countries met in the Coral Sea. When the air battle was over, Japan and the United States had each lost ships, and other vessels had been severely damaged. The Japanese had also lost a great many planes, so they gave up the Port Moresby attack and their plan to carry the war farther south or into Polynesia. Allied supply lines between North America and Australia remained open throughout the war.

Although unable to spread the war as far as Polynesia, Japan did try to jump from Micronesia to the doorstep of Hawaii. In June 1942, Japanese ships and planes made a major attack against Midway, which is actually a part of the mountain chain that makes up the Hawaiian Islands. Because the Americans had warning of the coming threat, they were able to prevent another Pearl Harbor. The defending force on Midway was weak, but the American planes got into the air and disrupted the Japanese attack. One after another of the United States planes was shot down, yet they kept the Japanese occupied while American aircraft carriers rushed to the scene. The planes from these ships scored direct hits on the Japanese vessels and turned a defensive battle into an important victory for the United States.

The battles of the Coral Sea and Midway had significance beyond protecting New Guinea and Hawaii. They gave a great boost to American morale, both at home and overseas, by proving that Japan's navy and air force could be beaten. They also showed the world that sea warfare had changed. Even though both sides used ships, the surface vessels never once bombarded one another. Planes did the attacking. The Coral Sea and Midway battles showed that the day of ship against ship had passed.

The Battle of Guadalcanal

In losing four aircraft carriers, more than two hundred planes, and over two thousand men at Midway alone, Japan lost a powerful striking force. At the same time she also weakened herself by extending the war almost to India and southward through Indonesia as well as into Melanesia, making it necessary to send men and supplies to many places over great distances. At the same time, American submarines made it increasingly difficult for Japanese ships to move freely in Oceania.

Allied leaders felt the time had now arrived for recapturing lost territory. They decided to launch their first offensive against Guadalcanal, in the Solomons, where the Japanese were building an airstrip and other defenses. American Marines landed on August 7, 1942, and soon captured the airstrip. After that, hanging on proved to be the real task. Unused to jungle and swamp fighting, the men found it difficult to locate enemy soldiers. Malaria added to their troubles.

The Japanese rushed troops from Rabaul, New Britain, their main base in the area. However, American ships and submarines stood by to try to prevent the landing of reinforcements. Through September,

October, and November fighting raged, sometimes on land, sometimes at sea. During this time, Americans learned much they needed to know about island warfare.

Both sides lost heavily toward the end of November, and they spent December recovering. During that time, the American land forces on Guadalcanal had one decided advantage: No Japanese vessels prevented their getting food from the south. The New Hebrides and New Caledonia provided supplies, and ships brought food from Australia and New Zealand as well. By contrast, the Japanese troops on Guadalcanal knew periods of near starvation. The fighting had destroyed everything on the island that might have been of use to them, and the American ships often kept their supplies from reaching them. By mid-January the Japanese, weakened by hunger, could not hold back an American drive to sweep them from Guadalcanal.

An Island-to-Island War

After taking Guadalcanal in February 1943, the Americans started the island-hopping techniques that would eventually carry them to the Ryukyu Islands in the western Pacific. On the way, it took them more than half a year to clear the central Solomons and almost another half year to gain control of Bougainville in the north. The Solomons were so torn up by the war that agriculture there took several years to recover. Even so, the Solomon Islanders helped the Americans. They had been virtual slaves under the Japanese, and the Allies promised them freedom once the war had passed out of their lands.

Not waiting for the Melanesian phase of the war to end, United States forces landed in the Ellice Islands. With the easy capture of Funafuti, headquarters of the Japanese in that group, they now readied an attack on the more heavily fortified islands of Tarawa and Makin in the northern Gilberts. After pounding the islands with bombs, the Americans landed on November 21, 1943.

Makin soon fell, but Tarawa presented unexpected difficulties. The landing craft became grounded on coral reefs around the island and

Unloading landing craft at Bougainville.

made it necessary for the Marines to wade a considerable distance in the face of heavy enemy fire. From this, the Americans learned to destroy or avoid such reefs in future landings on other islands. In addition, the original aerial bombardment had not been strong enough to weaken the hold of the Japanese force occupying the island. The invaders had to fight from tree to tree and from bunker to bunker, seeking an enemy that preferred to die rather than surrender. The Americans had to kill almost every Japanese on the island to gain control of it.

The War in the Marianas

Leap-frogging over the nearest islands in the Marshalls, the Americans took Kwajalein in February 1944. If they could take one of the westernmost Marshalls—Eniwetok—they would be within striking distance of the Marianas. In that way they could bypass the well-fortified islands of the Carolines, such as Ponape and Truk, although they bombed those bases to keep the Japanese ships and planes that were

Soldiers could smile for the camera even while digging in on Eniwetok.

stationed there from interfering with the Eniwetok invasion. After landing on Eniwetok, the Americans had to drive the enemy from their hiding places with grenades and flamethrowers.

The attack on the Marianas started with the bombing of the largest island, Saipan, on June 11, and troops went ashore four days later. Heavy fighting followed as the Marines fought off suicidal waves of Japanese. By this time, many of Japan's experienced fliers had been killed. The young men who replaced them had little training, and American antiaircraft gunners could easily shoot them from the skies. That made Allied attacks on Japanese ships easier, so the Marines invading Saipan had less than usual to worry about from the air or the sea.

In less than a month the Marines took Saipan, and in another month they captured Guam, but these victories would have been impossible at the time if General Douglas A. MacArthur had not had major Japanese forces occupied in trying to defend the Philippines.

The Beginning of the End of the War

The fall of the Marianas weakened Japanese morale considerably. The people of Japan looked on these islands as part of their homeland, and for the first time they realized that the war could reach their shores. From airbases in the Marianas, less than a thousand miles from Tokyo, B-29 bombers began to drop explosives on Japanese cities.

To the Americans, however, the Marianas lay far short of the Japanese homeland. They took the time to capture Peleliu, in the Palaus, because the Japanese had turned it into a major base after the destruction of Truk, and then they began the attack on the Volcano and Ryukyu islands.

The Allies might have done better to move north immediately, before the Japanese had time to strengthen their fortifications in the Volcanos. The central Japanese stronghold there was Iwo Jima, a dot of land less than eight miles square. When the Marines landed on it on February 19, 1945, the Japanese shot down at them from caves on the mountain slopes. The Marines suffered an alarming number of casualties before the island fell to them four weeks later.

Landing on Okinawa in the Ryukyu Islands on the first of April, the Americans met weak resistance at first, but a week later the Japanese counterattacked savagely. Fortunately for the Americans, the Japanese ships coming to support the land forces were defeated by American bombers. Having almost no navy left, Japan relied on planes to support the ground troops and tried to wipe out the Allied ships with *kamikaze,* or suicide raids. *Kamikaze* means "divine wind," and was first used as a name for a typhoon that destroyed a Chinese fleet sent against Japan seven hundred years ago. A *kamikaze* pilot made no attempt to bomb an American ship. Instead, he used his whole plane as a bomb, diving it directly into the ship. Such raids inflicted heavy damage, but not enough to drive off support for the American forces on Okinawa.

When Okinawa fell late in June, nearly 15,000 Americans had been killed and more than 35,000 wounded. If victory on one small island could take such a toll, what would the invasion of Japan cost? President Harry S Truman refused to find out. In August 1945, he authorized the use of atomic bombs on two Japanese cities, and the war in the Pacific came to an end.

After the United Nations came into existence, it made Micronesia a trust territory under the United States. The Ryukyus, Bonins, and Volcanos also came under United States jurisdiction, although Japan has since got parts of them back by peaceful means. She intends to regain them all someday, and some observers feel that she still has designs on Micronesia as well.

Parts of Melanesia became trust territories or colonies under Britain and Australia after the war, and France retained the islands that were already considered part of her overseas territory. On some islands, Japanese soldiers remained in hiding for years, living on wild fruits and nuts. Two were found on Guam in 1960; others have turned up in Saipan and Peleliu; and one gave up as recently as 1972. None of them could believe Japan had surrendered.

Recovering from the war, Oceania again became three separate regions, no longer united by a common enemy. However, they are not as distinct from one another as the names Polynesia, Melanesia, and Micronesia seem to imply.

Wreckage of an American plane on Guadalcanal.

A Japanese gun could still be seen in the Gilberts in the late 1960's.

Polynesia Today

Hawaii lies at the northern point of the Polynesian triangle. New Zealand forms the southwestern point, and Easter Island can be called the extremity of the southeast. Since these islands are being excluded from coverage in this book, Tahiti, the Samoas, and the Tongas remain as the best-known places in Polynesia, while the hundreds of other islands in the area richly earn it the name "Many Islands."

Tahiti, Capital of French Polynesia

We hear so much about Tahiti that many people think it is a group of islands. Actually, it is the main island of the Society group and the seat of government for all of French Polynesia. About half the people of French Polynesia live on Tahiti, and almost a fourth of all of them occupy the capital city of Papeete. Since Papeete itself has a population of fewer than 20,000, that means that all of French Polynesia has only 75,000 to 80,000 people. Taking a census in Oceania proves difficult, however, so figures are never exact.

Tahiti has an hourglass, or figure-eight, shape, with one section considerably larger than the other. This contour resulted when two volcanoes raised enough land between them to form a narrow connecting bridge. Associated with Tahiti are Moorea and Bora Bora, each of which has supporters who call it the most beautiful island in the world. Less well known in the Societies are Tahaa, Raiatéa, Huahiné, and a few others.

Being tall, this Polynesian of Tonga has to stoop under the banana ripening shed.

Bora Bora has a rugged beauty.

Makatea, although governed as part of the Societies, is geographically part of the Tuamotu Archipelago. That causes no conflict, however, because the Tuamotus are also in French Polynesia, as are other nearby groups—the Tubuai Islands, the Gambiers, and the Marquesas.

The French themselves don't look upon their part of Polynesia as a colony. They consider it an overseas section of their nation. Men of French descent whose families have lived in Polynesia for several generations think of themselves as local people rather than as Europeans and refuse to understand why men of Polynesian descent still see them as outsiders.

After the First World War, native Tahitians began demanding self-government. They won small concessions in the villages, but officials in positions of real power still came from France.

World War II helped the local cause a little. Some Tahitians fought alongside the French, and they felt that this earned them the right to be treated as equals. When the French showed little interest in their demands, they banded together to form a political party and elected a representative to sit in the National Assembly in Paris. Nevertheless, the governor of the island and his assistants remained French, and in 1958 the members of the territorial assembly in Papeete voted to let France continue to handle the administration of the government.

Members of the assembly are elected by popular vote, and both men and women have the right to cast a ballot. As the local political groups became stronger, people of Polynesian descent gained more seats in the assembly. In February 1969, they voted more than two to one for increased self-government—an indication that the people were becoming

The territorial assembly building of French Polynesia.

increasingly dissatisfied with having their region considered a section of France.

A few months later, the French Defense Ministry in Paris called off hydrogen-bomb tests that had been scheduled to take place in the Society Islands. Undoubtedly, the French did that in an effort to lessen tensions, but they did not go so far as to remove the French governor and other French officials from their posts.

Sooner or later, of course, the people of French Polynesia will achieve self-government, but that will not lead to a complete break with France. The economy of the islands is still linked too closely to the mother country for separation.

The Marquesas

Next to the Society Islands, the best-known islands in French Polynesia are probably the eleven Marquesas. Like the Societies, they are of volcanic origin and generally have narrow shoreline areas that give way to mountainous interiors, over which heavy clouds frequently hang.

The Marquesas are divided into two groups. The northern one includes Nuku Hiva, Ua Huka, and Ua Pou, with the seat of government on Nuku Hiva. To the south are Hiva Oa, Tahuata, Motane, and Fatu Hiva, governed from Hiva Oa.

The total area of the islands comes to slightly less than four hundred square miles, or about a quarter of French Polynesia. When the French took control of the Marquesas in 1842, the population came to about twenty thousand people, but European diseases decimated their numbers. Today four of the islands and several of the islets of the Marquesas have no inhabitants at all, and the population of most of the others can be numbered in the hundreds. The total comes to only about three thousand people, which is a very small part of French Polynesia.

The people of the Marquesas belong to several tribes, and each group wants to remain independent of the others. Before white men arrived, each tribe occupied its own mountain valley and ventured out only

A phosphate mine and shipping port in the Tuamotus.

when periods of drought, which occur more often in the Marquesas Islands than in most other parts of Oceania, affected the crops.

Today outsiders seldom live on these islands unless business keeps them there. Although handfuls of Chinese, who have become the restaurant and small-shop operators of Oceania, remain the year round, others prefer to live on Tahiti and go to the Marquesas only when their affairs demand it.

Tuamotu and the Gambiers

South of the Marquesas the Tuamotu ("Cloud of Islands") Archipelago forms a string stretching over a thousand miles along the eastern edge of French Polynesia. The Gambiers, lying at its southern end, can be considered a part of the archipelago even though they have their own seat of government. The Tuamotus are supervised from Apataki. The administrator of the Gambiers lives on the island of Mangareva.

The Tuamotus have a population of eight thousand to nine thousand, which would amount to about a hundred people to each island if all of them had occupants. Most of them don't, though, because they are not the most pleasant place in the world to live. Being low coral atolls and reefs, they have a poor sandy soil and suffer continually from strong winds and breakers. During typhoons, people sometimes have to climb trees to keep forty-foot waves from sweeping them out to sea. Only coconut and pandanus trees and occasional underbrush can survive on most of these atolls.

The seventy-five to eighty islands of the French Tuamotus have an area of about 335 square miles. Much of this area is the water in the central lagoon of each atoll. One of the main atolls, Takaroa, boasts a lagoon twelve miles long cut off from the ocean by a ring of sixteen islets.

The Gambiers make up a very small part of the archipelago. They consist of four inhabited islands, plus about a dozen others without permanent residents. The four main islands lie inside a protecting circle of reef. Here fewer than a thousand people occupy twelve square miles.

Thor Heyerdahl, on the research raft *Kon-Tiki*, grounded on Raroia Reef of the Tuamotus. He hoped to prove that the early peoples of Polynesia could have come from South America, but perhaps he only proved that the archipelago stands like a barrier along eastern Polynesia. Nevertheless, a surprising number of early navigators missed that barrier, which reminds us that eighty small islands scattered across a thousand miles have to be rather widely spaced.

The Tuamotus, including the Gambiers, became French after Catholic missionaries carried Christianity to the islands in the 1830's. The French annexed both groups formally in 1881, linking them for government purposes with the Society Islands.

The Tubuai Islands

Least known of the islands in French Polynesia, the Tubuais lie south of the Society Islands and west of the Gambiers. When the French annexed the Tubuais in 1880, they found the people little changed from when Captain Cook discovered one island, Tubuai, in 1777. Even by the third decade of the twentieth century, two of the four main islands had had so few outside visitors that the inhabitants were still of pure Polynesian stock and were among the healthiest people in the South Pacific. To keep them that way, the French discouraged travel to the islands. But during the 1960's, with modern medicines available to help the people, the territorial government lifted travel restrictions.

Estimates say about four thousand people—farmers and fishermen— live in the islands today, and, except for them, the Tubuai group is very similar to other Pacific islands. Volcanoes created Rimatara, Rurutu, Tubuai, and Raivavaé, but uninhabited Maria Island is of coral origin. Tropical plants flourish, and it takes little effort for a man to produce a satisfactory crop of taro, which is a major food in the Pacific.

Separated from the Tubuais, but linked with them for administrative purposes, are Rapa Island and the Bass Isles to the southeast. The Bass Islands have no permanent residents, but about three hundred fishermen occupy Rapa.

The Wallis and Futuna Islands

The French control two other small groups of islands occupied by Polynesians. Known as the Wallis and Futuna, or Hoorn, Islands, they fall between the zigzagging International Date Line and the 180th meridian. Because of this position, we might consider them Melanesian if the people didn't clearly show the characteristics of Polynesians.

At one time France associated these islands with the Societies, but later linked them with New Caledonia in Melanesia. They are more than a thousand miles from either place, but lie about seven hundred miles closer to New Caledonia than to Tahiti.

The people of the Wallis and Futuna groups dislike being governed from New Caledonia, because they prefer being associated with other Polynesians. Also, they want to become an overseas territory of France like French Polynesia instead of remaining a French protectorate. In 1959 a large majority of the people voted in favor of territorial status, but France has stalled on giving it to them. The Wallis and Futuna Islands remain under the French high commissioner for the Pacific, who also happens to be the governor of New Caledonia, where he spends most of his time.

The total population of the islands may not come to ten thousand people, and most of them live on the volcanic islands of Uvea, in the Wallis Islands, and Futuna, in the Futuna Islands. The total area of the group of islands comes to about seventy-five square miles, most of them consisting of uninhabited coral atolls.

British Claims to Polynesia

At one time or another, Britain has had some association with most of the islands of Polynesia. In certain areas she lost out to France, and she turned other sections over to New Zealand. In parts of the region, even today, the United States disputes Britain's claim to a number of islands. However, that still leaves a few places that can be considered strictly

Kingman Reef.

British. One of these areas is an extension of the Tuamotu Archipelago. At the southern end of the archipelago rise four dots of land—Oeno, Pitcairn, Henderson, and Ducie.

Only Pitcairn is inhabited, being home for a hundred or so people descended from the *Bounty* mutineers. Two or three goats for every person occupy about half the island. Having an area of only two square miles, Pitcairn hardly furnishes land enough for the people, but at one time their ancestors had a chance to live elsewhere and came back of their own accord.

All adults take a hand in the government of Pitcairn. They elect five of their number to act as the island council, while the rest belong to the general assembly. In time, their island may cease to be a colony and become an independent land within the British Commonwealth. In 1970, Queen Elizabeth II granted Pitcairn Island a coat of arms. The design included the *Bounty* Bible, the *Bounty* anchor, a wheelbarrow (major vehicle on the island), and a sprig from the miro tree, which provides carvers of Pitcairn with their best wood. Some people hope that the coat of arms indicates that the island is on its way toward full independence.

The Line Islands

The Line Islands stretch north from the Tuamotu Archipelago toward Hawaii. These coral atolls reach across the equator, which is the "line" that gives them their name.

The islands of Flint, Caroline, Vostok, Starbuck, Malden, and Christmas are all claimed by both Britain and the United States. Washington and Fanning belong to Britain, though discovered by an American, Edmund Fanning. Jarvis, Palmyra, and Kingman Reef are undisputedly American.

Several of the islands have areas of less than a square mile and no inhabitants. There were no inhabitants on any of the islands when the Americans discovered them in 1798, but they were covered with rich guano deposits. Since then decades of mining have reduced the guano considerably. Today the islands remain of importance for air and naval bases.

Fanning serves the British Commonwealth as a station for an undersea cable stretching from Canada's west coast to New Zealand, and Britain has tested atomic devices on Christmas and Malden.

Christmas is the largest island of the group as well as the largest atoll in the Pacific. With a land area of about 225 square miles, it makes up nearly half the territory of the Line Islands. However, it falls far short of having half the population, because fewer than a hundred people live there. Fanning has the most people, about four hundred, and Washington is next with two hundred. The three American islands have about a hundred people altogether, half of them on Palmyra.

The Phoenix Islands

Another area claimed by both the United States and Britain, the Phoenix Islands, extends west of the Line Islands almost to the International Date Line. Like the Lines, they resulted from coral activity, lacked appeal for early settlers, and once held abundant guano deposits. In the late 1930's, colonizers from the Gilberts came to the Phoenix Islands, making their homes on Hull, Sydney, and Gardner. By 1968, having found these islands unsatisfactory for comfortable living, many of the newcomers had abandoned them.

All but two of the eight islands in the Phoenix group, as well as Christmas (despite the United States claim), Fanning, and Washington in the Line Islands, fall under the jurisdiction of the British Gilbert and Ellice Islands colony. Britain and the United States govern Canton and Enderbury jointly, as a condominium. The total area of the Phoenix Islands amounts to eleven square miles, and the population comes to less than a thousand.

Tokelau and Manihiki and the Cook Islands

Just south of the Phoenix Islands is the Tokelau, or Union, group, discovered by John Byron in 1765. The three Tokelaus and associated

If it weren't for the trees, the low-lying Tokelaus would be difficult to see.

islets cover about five square miles and provide a home for about two thousand people, who live by farming and selling copra. These coral islands came under New Zealand's administration when it took over Western Samoa, and are now considered a part of New Zealand.

Somewhat east and south of the Tokelaus lie atolls sometimes considered together as the Manihiki Islands. They include Puka Puka, Nassau, Penrhyn, Rakahanga, and Manihiki. Near them is Suvorov (Suwarrow) Island. Since Americans discovered Manihiki in 1822, all of them have been claimed by the United States at one time or another, but today they, too, are governed by New Zealand and share an administrator with the Cook Islands, six hundred miles to the south.

The Cooks are mostly atolls but have two important volcanic islands, Rarotonga and Mangaia. They could have had their independence in 1962, but, while the people chose to take local government into their own hands, they decided to leave international affairs to New Zealand. With the Manihiki group, the total population of the Cook Islands comes to about sixteen thousand people, scraping a living from a land area of about a hundred square miles.

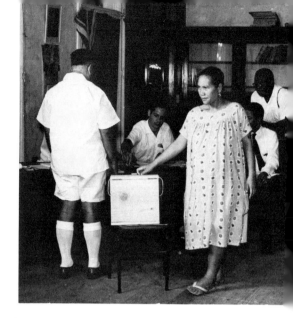

United Nations representatives have supervised major elections in the Cook Islands, which New Zealand considers to be independent.

American Islands in Polynesia

Besides the three small atolls in the Line Islands, the United States can make full claim to three little islands that are free of association with any group. Just north of the Phoenix Islands are Baker and Howland. Baker serves as a naval base but has no permanent population. Guano deposits there once produced revenue, as did those on Howland, forty miles north.

Howland gained inhabitants in the mid-1930's, when Hawaiians came there to take up land. The United States Department of the Interior administers Howland. It and Baker have an area of about one square mile apiece.

The third separate island, Johnston, lies closer to Hawaii than it does to any other region. When Hawaii existed as an independent kingdom, it claimed the atoll as part of its territory. The United States, however, keeps it separate, placing it under the jurisdiction of the Navy. Consisting of two coral islets protected by a reef, Johnston has less than a square mile of land area. Its few dozen residents look after a landing field and naval installations. When the United States Army removed supplies of mustard gas, a military weapon, from Okinawa in 1971, it shipped them to Johnston for storage.

84

American Samoa

More important than the above American islands and the jointly claimed atolls is American Samoa. Because the United States considered Pago Pago Harbor on Tutuila to be strategic, it kept the possession under Navy control for half a century. During that time the islanders objected more and more, claiming the military regime gave little consideration to the needs and desires of the Samoan people. Many faults could be found with the way the islands were governed. Although the United States did bring medical care to them and introduced six grades of schooling, the naval personnel often acted as if they were outside the jurisdiction of the law, and much of the time they treated the Samoans as inferiors.

Finally, in 1951, President Truman transferred the administration of the islands to the Department of the Interior, which promised the people a constitution. It was nine years in the making. When at last the people got their constitution, they began to hope for self-government. That, too, is in the making, but some Samoans have shown a lack of interest in democratic procedures, which causes practically everyone to drag his feet.

In 1970, however, a political status commission recommended that the twenty thousand American Samoans elect their governor. Up to now the governor has been appointed by the President of the United States, and until the 1950's all the administrators came from the States. Then Peter T. Coleman, son of an American sailor and a Samoan woman, was given the appointment. That pleased many of the people, even though he resembled Americans in much of his thinking. When he earned a degree in law from Georgetown University, Washington, D. C., he became the first Samoan to be a degree-holding lawyer. In 1961, the Department of the Interior transferred him to Micronesia, where he has held high-ranking posts in the Marshalls and the Marianas.

Under the American Samoa governor, three district governors hold office, and all of them are local people. Below them come county chiefs, then village chiefs, and finally headmen. Headmen are usually heads of large family groups and are sometimes called talking chiefs. They have the most direct contact with the people, passing along to all the relatives under them the rules that come down from the chiefs higher up on the scale.

In addition to chiefs, there is a *Fono,* or legislature. Members of the upper house are elected by the chiefs from among their own ranks. All adults cast secret ballots to chose the members of the lower house, to which a man other than a chief can seek election. The *Fono* gained power in the 1960's and is now the strongest part of the Samoan government.

American Samoa has an official representative in the United States Congress in Washington. This delegate-at-large post came into existence in 1970, and the first election to fill it occurred in November of that year. Besides filling the post, it was the first election in the territory that allowed all adults in American Samoa to vote. High Chief A. U. Fuimaono won. Before that he had been director of agriculture.

Although having a native-born governor and a delegate-at-large satisfies some of the people's desires, they want more changes. They would still like to be self-governing citizens of the United States, as the people of Puerto Rico are, or else achieve statehood. However, American Samoa pays less than half the expense of operating its government, so it can't really support self-government. The territory has a fast-growing population, making it necessary to build houses on acres formerly used for crops. The land that once provided an abundance of taro, arrowroot, yams, pineapples, papayas, mangoes, and coconuts for the people now fails to feed them adequately.

Young people, which means practically everyone under fifty, want more say in running American Samoa. In the past, people assumed that wisdom came with age, so all the chiefs were old men. That practice has continued into the present. In Samoa a man of sixty or seventy receives more respect than one of fifty to sixty, while a "lad" of twenty to forty has little hope of joining the ruling class for years.

American movies and the youthful officers they see on American ships have made the young Samoans conscious of some lack of logic in their old system—and with its fast-growing population, American Samoa has a mass of youth that becomes more vocal every year. Some of the current chiefs must be quaking with fear as well as with old age, for world patterns show that youth can bring changes.

American Samoa divides roughly into three areas. Tutuila is the main island, and it is there and on its tiny neighbor Aunuu that American influence has been strongest. These two islands have lost many of their ancient customs.

Continuing more in the pattern of the past is the Manua group, three small islands to the east, whose total area is less than Tutuila's forty-two square miles. Rose Island, an uninhabited coral atoll, is associated with them.

The third region of American Samoa, Swains Island to the north, is really a geographic part of the Tokelaus, but it is linked to Tutuila for administrative purposes because of American control.

The main street along the waterfront of Apia, Western Samoa.

American Samoa is only thirty-six miles from Western Samoa, a very small distance in the Pacific. Geographically, both regions are formed by volcanic mountaintops rising from the same ocean-floor plateau. American Samoa's highest peak, on Tau Island, reaches slightly over 2,000 feet, and Western Samoa has a peak more than 6,000 feet high on Savaii Island. The climate of both groups is the same except in the high places, with more than a hundred inches of rainfall a year and temperatures that average close to 80 degrees Fahrenheit. In Samoa, as throughout Oceania, dampness seeps into everything, making it necessary to keep light bulbs burning in closets to prevent mildew.

Not only are the two Samoas much alike physically, their people are alike too—or were until outsiders of different backgrounds took them over. American Samoans on Tutuila have changed the most by adopting many American ways.

Western Samoa

Because of the common background of the two Samoas, Western Samoan politicians seek to unite American Samoa with their own country. But many Samoans in the American section prefer the present division. American Samoa, with its 76 square miles, can't compare in size with either Upolu (430 square miles) or Savaii (703 square miles). The eastern islands, with their 25,000 people, would probably become minor elements in a united Samoa that included the 150,000 people of Western Samoa. As it now stands, the American territory enjoys a certain prominence and also fares better financially than many parts of Polynesia.

Western Samoa became the first independent nation in Polynesia after New Zealand. Following World War II, New Zealand prepared it for freedom because it appeared that the trust territory could manage its own affairs. On January 1, 1962, the independent nation of Western Samoa came into existence, although it isn't actually as free as it likes to think. A tourist or foreign businessman visiting the country today must still obtain a visa or make other arrangements through a New Zealand

Western Samoa's Parliament building resembles a Samoan house.

consulate abroad. If another war struck the Pacific, Western Samoa would need considerable help from outsiders to protect herself.

Two chiefs, Malietoa Tanumafili II and Tupua Tamaseso, were the logical choices for a head of state when the country became free. They had been especially active in leading the nation to self-government, and rather than accept one and anger the other, New Zealand allowed them to share the honor of heading the government. However, when one of them dies, his heirs will not gain his place. Instead, the one who remains alive will then be head of state by himself for five years. After that, elections will decide the leader at five-year intervals.

In Western Samoa, though, it is the prime minister rather than the head of state who holds the real power. The first prime minister, another man of prominence from a long line of chiefs, was Fiame Mataáfa.

When choosing freedom, Western Samoa rejected some of the democratic practices of New Zealand. In the past, the *matai,* or head of a family, spoke for the relatives under him. Western Samoans preferred to keep this practice rather than give the vote to all adults. As a result, in a land of nearly 150,000 people, of which perhaps 70,000 might be old enough to vote, fewer than 10,000 cast ballots.

Young people began to object to this practice in the mid-1960's. By 1969, they had complained loudly enough for the legislative assembly to consider extending suffrage to all adults, but the proposal was defeated by a vote of better than five to one. Since assembly members are mainly old men, the outcome hardly gives a trustworthy view of what the people in general desire. Along with American Samoa, the western islands have the fastest-growing population in Polynesia, and more than half the citizens are in their teens or younger. It must be only a matter of time until the *matai* system falls, and men between twenty-five and fifty have more say in national affairs.

Outsiders hardly realize that Western Samoa consists of nine islands rather than two. Because Upolu and Savaii make up most of the land area, the tiny islets between them and around Upolu can easily be overlooked. Out of the country's 1,130 square miles, the islets have about a square mile among them. Fishermen visit them, but few of them have permanent inhabitants. Upolu has more than half the nation's population, with thirty thousand or so living in the capital, Apia.

The house of a village chief in the Samoas frequently stands out.

The Royal Palace of Tonga, in Nukualofa.

Tonga

Following Western Samoa's lead, Tonga, or the Friendly Islands, which lie between the Cook Islands and Fiji, became independent in 1970.

Tonga has probably been settled since 400 B.C., and claims to be the world's oldest monarchy, having had a king since before the time of recorded history. The present royal family dates back to 1845, when a chief put an end to a civil war and thereafter called himself King George Tupou I. Influenced by the government of Great Britain, he gave the people a constitution in 1862.

British influence has been strong in Tonga ever since the arrival of London Missionary Society members in 1797 and the Wesleyans twenty-five years later. In 1901, King Tupou II ratified a treaty with Britain that made the nation a British protectorate. A British representative thereafter approved all legislation and financial plans, although in matters of local interest, he allowed Tongan officials and legislators full authority.

Tonga gained prominence in 1953, when Queen Salote Tupou went to England for Queen Elizabeth II's coronation. For one thing, Queen Salote was more than six feet tall. In addition, her regal bearing and refined manners captured the attention and admiration of everyone present. Salote died in 1965, and her son Taufa'ahau Tupou IV became king. His monarchy contains only 270 square miles, spread over 150 to 200 islands.

Actually, Tonga's independence somewhat resembles Western Samoa's. The Tongans cannot afford to manage their affairs without outside help, and many of them would have been content to remain in a semi-independent situation if their main rival, Melanesia's Fiji, had not been slated for freedom.

Tonga had already fallen behind Fiji in one respect. Fiji's international airport, at Nandi, was enlarged in the 1960's to handle jet planes, so the Tongans made plans for a jetport too. King Taufa'ahau Tupou IV turned to Britain for financial aid, but Britain refused, and shortly after that, in 1969, the king announced that his nation would become independent in 1970. In 1971, Tonga went ahead with plans to equip her airport to handle jets.

Today in Tonga, a prime minister heads a seven-man cabinet, or council, of his and the king's choosing. The legislative assembly includes the seven in the cabinet plus fourteen other men. Seven of the fourteen are nobles elected by a vote of all the nobles, and the remaining seven legislators are elected by all males over twenty-one who can read and write and who pay taxes.

When the monarch is present, everyone else sits or stands when he does. Foreigners who don't know local etiquette will be asked to comply or to depart the royal presence. Many soccer matches take place on a lawn just across a low wall from the royal palace. If the king comes to the wall and stands watching, any seated spectators jump to their feet. If he drives by in his car and has the driver stop so he can watch, all the people standing around the playing area immediately squat on the ground as long as he remains seated in his car. At church, the people stand when he enters the royal pew and sit as soon as he sits. Late arrivals find a seat and sit as quickly as possible if he is already in his place. The current king attends church every Sunday that he is in Nukualofa, the capital. In his absence his brother, who is prime minister, occupies the royal pew.

Nukualofa is a small city spread along a cape on the northern coast of Tongatapu, the country's largest island. About half of Tonga's 65,000 people live on Tongatapu, with 20,000 of them in the capital itself. Nukualofa had dirt or turf-covered roads until the mid-1960's, but now a few main streets are hard surfaced for at least a few blocks. Most of the other settlements on the islands are villages, situated mainly on Tongatapu, Haabai, or Vavau. The country is still primitive away from

The main street hardly makes Nukualofa appear to be a capital city.

Two women of Niue cut pandanus leaves to use in weaving baskets, a major industry of the island.

the centers of population, although Tongatapu has a good network of roads for an island of Oceania. A few islands at the southwestern end of the country, including Tongatapu, are considered volcanic. However, at places along their coasts great stretches of coral exist, and most of the islands of the country are coralline in origin.

Minerva Reef, south of Tongatapu, is one of the most dreaded coral stretches in Polynesia. Exposed only at low tide, it grounds ships that fail to locate its markers after dark or during storms. The Tongans fear it so much that they won't willingly go out to it even to save cargo. When a New Zealand vessel plowed into Minerva Reef in the fall of

1970, the company owning the ship immediately flew a representative to Tonga. This outside supervisor finally collected a crew and rescued some of the cargo, but all of it would have gone to the bottom if it had been up to the local people to go out after it on their own.

Niue—the Savage Island

Just east of the northern Tongas, a mountain peak known as Niue rises out of the ocean. When Captain Cook discovered it in 1774, he called it Savage Island because the people proved unfriendly. By contrast, the year before, he had received a kindly welcome from the Tongans and had named their group the Friendly Islands.

New Zealand claimed Niue's one hundred square miles in 1901 and briefly included it with the Cook Islands. Since 1903 it has been administered by its own people, who are working toward self-government. They held their first elections in 1969. An airfield, started in 1969, made the six thousand or so Niuans hope for a growing tourist business in the future.

Some Tongans think the island should be part of their country, but the people of Niue, who show more Melanesian characteristics than Tongans do, generally disagree.

The side of the imaginary Polynesian triangle that runs from Hawaii to New Zealand practically cuts the Lau Islands in two, but long ago the warlike Fijians took control of the Laus, so they belong in Melanesia rather than Polynesia. From Tonga in southwestern Polynesia, it is a short jump—about two hundred miles—to Fiji in southeastern Melanesia.

Modern Melanesia

Melanesia has probably had more cannibals and head hunters than any other part of Oceania. Possibly even in the twentieth century, head-hunting and people-eating have persisted in certain regions, especially New Guinea, the Solomons, and Fiji.

All of Melanesia lies south of the equator and west of the International Date Line. It reaches as far west as Indonesia, although it doesn't include that country. Melanesia does include New Guinea, half of which belongs to Indonesia. The other half is part of an Australian colony and trust territory. Since New Guinea is frequently discussed in books on Indonesia and Australia as well as by itself, it won't receive much attention here.

More space will be given to the part of the trust territory that includes the Bismarck Archipelago. One large and one small island of the Solomons also belong in the trust territory, although most of the Solomons form a separate region, with the Santa Cruz Islands at their southeastern tip. The Santa Cruz Islands lie north of the New Hebrides, which are themselves north of the Loyalties and New Caledonia. All of them lie west of the Fiji Islands, where many people show signs of having Polynesian blood and are lighter-skinned than the dark-brown inhabitants of most of Melanesia.

The New Hebrides need alert young men like this one in a World Health Organization program to work for a better tomorrow.

The Fiji Islands

Back in the days of cannibalism, a meal of "long pig" was one of human flesh. Small hot peppers and other vegetables were served with it to add flavor. In the 1860's a missionary named Thomas Baker became the main course in a "long pig" feast. It has been said that the Fijians boiled and tried to eat Baker's boots as well, but gave up when a chief broke a tooth on one of them.

The Fiji Islanders also offered up human life as a sacrifice during ceremonies, and in times of tribal warfare men captured in battle served as these sacrifices. That explains why the Fijians were such fierce warriors. Knowing they would die if captured, men fought to the death.

Levuka, the original capital of the Fijis, stood on Ovalau Island. In case of an invasion, the ruling chief and his supporters could seek safety on cliffs that rise just behind the village. During the nineteenth century, a chief named Thakombau (another spelling is Chakobau) became powerful. Thakombau adopted Christianity, mostly to get help from white men, many of whom had fled prisons in Australia and were looking for profit and power in the islands. With their assistance Thakombau forced his rule on most of the surrounding islands in a rather unchristian way.

However, Thakombau soon realized he couldn't hold his kingdom against a number of enemy chiefs, and he asked Queen Victoria for British protection. Her government turned him down, partly because of the reputation the Fijians had for eating people. A few years later Thakombau called on the United States for help, but Abraham Lincoln's government was involved in the Civil War and gave him no reply. Then, after missionaries began to stamp out cannibalism, Thakombau turned again to Britain and won his way. Fiji became a British protectorate in 1874, and most of the convicts behind Thakombau scuttled off to other islands. With British warships at hand, the chief felt that the mountains crowding down to the sea on Ovalau had ceased to serve any purpose and would keep Levuka from expanding, so he moved the capital to Suva.

Low buildings rather than high ones sprawl along Suva's industrial section.

The British government outlawed cannibalism, of course, and there is no official record of it after they took over. Nevertheless, in remote areas of Fiji it probably lasted for at least another thirty years and, in fact, rumors of the practice circulated until World War I.

The British made other changes besides outlawing human sacrifice and cannibalism. Especially far-reaching were the changes brought about by the sugar plantations they introduced.

A mountain range divides Fiji's largest island of Viti Levu into an eastern section, which receives much rain, and a drier western half. Sugarcane grows well on the moist side. The British hired the islanders to work in the cane fields, but for starvation wages, and the people gave as little service as they could get away with. As objections to slavery and blackbirding increased, the British began to hire laborers from India instead. Boatloads of East Indians came to Fiji. Happy to

99

A guard in traditional uniform paced before the entrance to Government House when a British governor lived there.

escape the crowded conditions at home, they worked off their indebtedness for transportation to Fiji and became citizens. As their numbers increased, they opened market stalls and small shops. At first none of this bothered the Fijians, who didn't guess that the East Indians would become the largest group in the islands.

Today there are more East Indians in the Fijis than there are Fijians. The Indians consider the islands their home and have no intention of returning to India. For work in their shops and on their garden plots, they hire other East Indians. In the same way, the Chinese who come to the islands hire other Chinese.

That leaves the Fijians to work for the British or for themselves, but most of them show little interest in starting or running businesses of their own. Fijians own 80 percent of the land, because the laws forbid outsiders to buy it, so they rent it to the East Indians, Chinese, and British. Numerous Fijians end up being servants in the homes of foreigners. Many hold positions as clerks in the government and in British businesses. Others live as fishermen, but inland villagers follow the ways of their ancestors and raise vegetables or look after coconut and other food-bearing trees.

Resentment has grown among the Fijians about the aggressiveness of the East Indians, although the Indians themselves frequently try to deny that any problems exist. As independence approached in 1970, the East Indians began to minimize or ignore the feeling against them. Perhaps they feared that unrest would postpone independence.

On the other hand the Fijians were afraid the Indians would grab control of the islands after they gained their freedom. As independence talks proceeded, more and more slogans, or graffiti, against the Indians appeared on walls. Some of the writing sounded quite angry, indicating a possibility of violence, in spite of the fact that most people in civilized areas of the Pacific are easygoing and peaceful.

Before independence came on October 10, 1970, a system of government had to be worked out that satisfied everyone living in the Fijis. In the past, a governor represented the British monarch and kept an eye on the legislative council. He appointed half its members, while the other half were elected by the people. Fijians made up one third of the council, East Indians constituted a third, and the other third came from among people of European descent. This gave Europeans a mighty big say in island affairs, considering the smallness of their population.

In the new parliament, based somewhat on Britain's, all the legislators are elected. Fijians and East Indians have equal say, and the Fijians count on support from a small number of non-East Indians to help them control the government.

The first prime minister of Fiji, Ratu K. K. T. Mara, received his advanced education in England, at Oxford. A tall, broad-shouldered man, he appeared to some outsiders like a rather dark Polynesian. Actually he is a Melanesian.

Of the 530,000 people in the Fiji Islands, more than half have East Indian ancestors. Another 240,000 are of Fijian descent. Perhaps 15,000 are European, and about an equal number have Chinese, Japanese, or other Asian blood. People from other islands of Oceania, especially from Tonga, live in the Fijis because educational and medical facilities exist there that are not found in many island communities.

Because of their international jet airport and the advanced condition of the country and the people, the Fijis receive more outside visitors than any of the other islands of Melanesia.

Throughout Oceania, however, few settlements except capital cities are equipped to handle visitors, and Fiji is no exception. Most tourists seldom see beyond its largest island, Viti Levu (Great Fiji), home of the capital city, Suva. There are two airports on Viti Levu, and only

A village of Uvea, one of the Loyalties, can hardly be seen from a distance because of coconut palms.

there do many roads exist. The main one runs around the coast of the island, and anyone wanting to get to an island village usually travels by motor-driven canoe, as most settlements stand beside streams.

Just northeast of Viti Levu, with its 4,010 square miles, is the island of Vanua Levu, which ranks second with an area of about 2,135 square miles. That means that Viti Levu and Vanua Levu make up most of the country, for the total area of Fiji amounts to only about 7,050 square miles.

More people live on Viti Levu than on any of the other 250 to 300 islands, and Suva is not only the capital, it is also the largest city, with about 25,000 people in town and as many more in the outskirts.

Suva has one small shop after another lined up along a few main streets, and business offices can be found either at street level or one flight up. Throughout Oceania as well as in Fiji buildings seldom reach a height of more than two or three stories. The British still operate the big businesses in Fiji, such as hotels, major stores, factories, and plantations, while most of Suva's small shops continue to have East Indian owners. Eating places are frequently run by Chinese, but "long pig" never appears on the menu.

New Caledonia and Its Neighbors

New Caledonia dominates the islands in its neighborhood. For one thing, with its area of about 8,850 square miles, it ranks among the largest islands of Oceania. For another thing, the capital city, Nouméa, has become the main administrative center of French islands in Melanesia. The other islands in the vicinity include the Loyalties, the Chesterfields, the Huons, the Béleps, Walpole Island, Nou Island, and the Isle of Pines. With New Caledonia, these make up an overseas territory of France amounting to about 9,400 square miles. The territory's 85,000 people live mainly on three of the Loyalties—Lifu, Uvéa, and Maré—the Isle of Pines, and New Caledonia.

Captain Cook discovered the volcanic island of New Caledonia and, thinking the northern coast resembled that of Scotland (Caledonia), provided its name. After that the British took little interest in it. Catholic missionaries finally came from France. In 1850, the local people killed the sailors of a French ship, giving France an excuse to land troops. Three years later France took possession.

The Isle of Pines, also discovered and named by Cook, was occupied by the French in 1850, and the main Loyalty Islands came under French control a year later. The other islands in the vicinity were mostly claimed during the next decade. France used Nou, a small island outside the excellent harbor of Nouméa, and the Isle of Pines as penal colonies. For the thirty years from 1864 to 1894 about 50,000 prisoners were shipped to the islands from jails in France, and today many New Caledonians of French descent can trace their ancestry back to these French criminals.

After World War II, France pursued a reasonably wise course in the islands making up its Melanesian territory. She conferred French citizenship on the people instead of treating them like a colony and gave voting privileges to all adult males able to read and write. Although some of the people had been forced to work during the Second World War, that policy was dropped when peace returned, and officials introduced modern methods and to some extent modern machinery in the mines essential to the territory's economy.

The voters, which today include women as well as men, elect members to a territorial assembly. These legislators serve five-year terms and, while in office, select from among themselves a cabinet, or advisory council, to assist the governor. The territory also sends a representative to Paris. As yet, the New Caledonians have not demanded as much freedom in government as the Tahitians have in French Polynesia.

Nouméa, the capital of New Caledonia, has an exotic air, being peopled by New Caledonians, Polynesians, Vietnamese, and Indonesians in addition to the French, who outnumber the others. Only in recent years have numerous local people moved into the capital, which has narrow tree-bordered streets like those of old cities in Asia.

Nouméa can be reached by air from Australia and Fiji, and the three

A modern nickel plant in New Caledonia.

largest Loyalty Islands have small-plane service from Nouméa. Ships connect many of the islands, though service may be irregular.

All settlements in the Loyalty Islands are villages, and the total population comes to about fifteen thousand. Many of the people there are Polynesian rather than Melanesian.

Unlike New Caledonia, these islands are coralline. However, some volcanic activity has raised the coral well above sea level in places. The Loyalties lie about sixty miles from New Caledonia and aren't much farther than that from the southernmost islands of the New Hebrides.

The New Hebrides Islands

Like New Caledonia, the New Hebrides mostly resulted from volcanic activity, and a few volcanoes remain active today. Only scattered

105

minor islets came from the building work of coral polyps. Of the nearly one hundred islands and islets, about thirty have occupants, and just a dozen of them are of much size or importance. The total area amounts to roughly 5,700 square miles, with the largest island, Espiritu Santo, making up a fourth of that. Important mainly for agriculture but with some nickel and iron mining, Espiritu Santo ranks second in importance to Efate, where the capital city of Vila is located. An unusual feature of the New Hebrides is that Vila is the location of not one, but two governments.

Queirós discovered the islands of the New Hebrides, but navigators who followed him couldn't find them after that, and they had to be discovered anew. Bougainville came along a century and a half later, giving France a claim, but Cook followed in a few years and named the islands. Another half century passed, and Catholic missionaries arrived from France. Soon after, Presbyterians came from Australia. Neither mission group would give way to the other, and when French and British merchants started visiting the islands, they complicated the situation further.

In the mid-1870's, France was still weak because of the Franco-Prussian War, and Britain had spread herself rather thin throughout the Pacific, Southeast Asia, India, Africa, and the West Indies. Neither country wanted war over small, mosquito-infested islands halfway around the world that stretched in a string more than four hundred miles long. They reached a pact that made the New Hebrides a neutral zone for nine years. Then, in 1887, they set up a joint control.

The first administration was a joint naval commission with the main obligations of keeping the people from creating civil war and of protecting the islands from other interested powers. After nineteen years of this uneasy naval control, the two nations agreed to a joint government, or condominium. They confirmed this arrangement at the start of World War I and reconfirmed it after formation of the League of Nations.

After the Second World War, the New Hebrides returned to normal more quickly than many other island groups because of the competition there between the French and British. Apparently the French thought they saw an opportunity to gain control of the business and commercial life of the islands. That forced the British to move with speed in returning their business interests to full operation.

During this activity, the rights and interests of the islanders often came up for discussion among the politicians and businessmen. Unfortunately there was more talk than action. When a law did pass to help the local people, outsiders ignored it if it interfered with their efforts to make profits.

The progress that followed the war began to lag in the years leading up to the 1970's. Today both France and Britain insist on having their own way in looking after the islands. Each has its own set of laws, its own currency, and its own educational system, so it is no wonder the New Hebrideans live in a state of confusion. They're afraid to use any of the money but can't get along without it. They have to try to keep track of everybody's rules, and they aren't sure whether their children are getting a useful education or not.

A New Hebridean has neither French nor British citizenship, and he can't even say that the island on which he lives is his own. The New Hebrideans, the French, and the British all say a change must be made, and in the meantime, missionaries are giving the people the courage to go on. They provide medical aid and legal or business advice and have brought to the New Hebrides the best system of education being offered.

Of the condominium's 60,000 people, Melanesians account for 50,000. Frenchmen number about 2,000 and British about half that, while nearly 3,000 of the islanders are from Southeast Asia, especially Vietnam. Most of the other 4,000 people come from other parts of Asia, Australia, New Zealand, and Polynesia.

Any one of these people will find it difficult to contact the head of either government. The Pacific high commissioner for the British islands heads the British system, but his headquarters are in the Solo-

After agriculture returned to normal in the Solomons, sorghum became an important crop.

mons. In charge of the French branch of the condominium is the governor of New Caledonia. The commissioners, who must answer to these men, live in Vila.

Even individual islands, such as Espiritu Santo, have separate local administrations. The British on Espiritu Santo have their offices in the north at Hog Harbour; the French govern from Segond Canal in the south. The 5,000 people of the island usually answer to whichever administration is nearer.

The Solomons

The world became particularly aware of the Solomons because of the World War II battles for Guadalcanal and Bougainville. After the war, the British colony recovered slowly. The land had been badly torn up, making farming difficult for several years. Many former landlords felt no responsibility to return from Europe and help improve conditions. Those who did come back had lost the respect of the local people, who had seen them flee like timid animals before the Japanese in the 1940's. The Solomon Island tribesmen had been a servant class before the war, but they asserted their independence when peace returned.

"Independence" for the people of the Solomons meant being allowed to live according to their tribal ways. It had little to do with setting up their own government and running it free of outside interference. When, early in the 1960's, the British introduced steps to prepare the local people for internal self-government, the islanders reacted with indifference. In the Solomons the people of one tribe seldom trust the people of another, so that anybody who claims he wants to improve conditions is treated with suspicion by almost everybody. As a result, progress toward self-rule has been so slow that the British find it impossible to predict when the islands will be ready to look after their

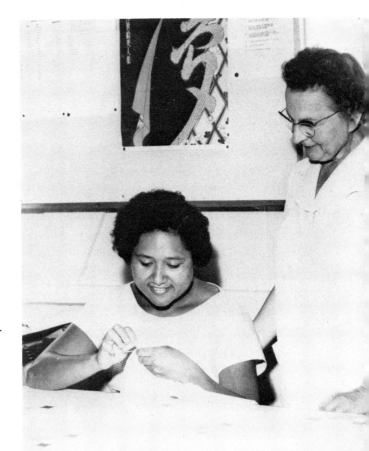

A Solomon Island girl learns to sew, helped by a Food and Agriculture Organization adviser. Her new knowledge will prove useful.

home affairs. Complete independence lies even farther in the future, if ever, because tribal life seems to suit the people best.

During the war, the Solomon Islanders became used to improved wages and working conditions. They were unwilling to accept prewar standards once peace returned, which led to constant conflicts with outsiders. In an effort to take matters into their own hands, some local politicians tried to form what they called self-help groups, and many tribesmen followed these leaders, expecting that everyone would benefit. As it turned out, a lot of the organizers thought only of their own gains so that, in 1947, most of them were arrested. After that the groups fell apart, leaving behind the suspicion that is hindering efforts to improve conditions today.

Undoubtedly some of the political leaders were capable men and could

Like boys everywhere, those of the Solomons enjoy climbing trees.

Many Melanesians, such as these men of New Britain being visited by United Nations advisers, are short.

have helped the people. The British recognized the need to sift them from the troublemakers and profiteers and to educate all the people to take part in political life. Therefore, they set up native councils to allow the tribesmen more say in their local affairs and to provide a training ground for men of promise, while themselves screening local politicians to find prospective leaders.

Generally the councils are organized along lines of tribal territories, the tribe for each region having its own council. If a tribe's gardens and trees produce adequately, it has no desire to occupy other land; it merely wants other groups to stay off its ground. In the same way, people along coasts or streams have fishing territories. The councils maintain this traditional division.

Where coconut and ivory nut trees grow wild, people can live without much effort. However, farming in the Solomon Islands requires harder work than in many places of the world. The numerous minor coral atolls there provide too shallow a soil for any kind of concentrated agriculture, and all of the ten or so major islands are volcanic and quite mountainous, with peaks up to ten thousand feet. In fact, the active volcanoes sometimes threaten to wipe out whole villages. Heavy rainfall and a rich soil on the volcanic islands stimulate jungle growth that can take over cleared land except where it rises too high or becomes too swampy. Mangrove swamps occupy the low coastal areas.

In the south, which includes the Santa Cruz group of about four main islands and half a dozen coral atolls, heat and humidity remain high the year round. Although farmers have adjusted to conditions in the Santa Cruz Islands they still face blackwater fever, which is a type of malaria, and dysentery. Fewer than 10,000 of the Solomons' 185,000 inhabitants live in the Santa Cruz Islands, and these southern islands make up only a small portion of the total area, accounting for 375 out of 15,100 square miles. The local administration operates from Peu on the largest island, Ndeni, also known as Santa Cruz.

Guadalcanal, with an area of 2,500 square miles, offers more space than the Santa Cruz Islands. Its population comes to about 20,000, and, except for a few hundred whites and handfuls of Chinese in the capital, most of the people are Melanesian.

The people of the Solomons are generally darker and shorter than those of Fiji, New Caledonia, and the New Hebrides, with many of the interior tribesmen being black. Pygmies can be found in the southern islands, while some of the darkest and tallest—almost "giants"—live in the north, especially on Bougainville.

Bougainville is the one island of the Solomons larger than Guadalcanal. With an area of 3,880 square miles and a population of 60,000, this island might be expected to dominate its group, but it has been separated from the other Solomons politically. Bougainville and nearby Buka fall within the Australian territory of Papua and New Guinea.

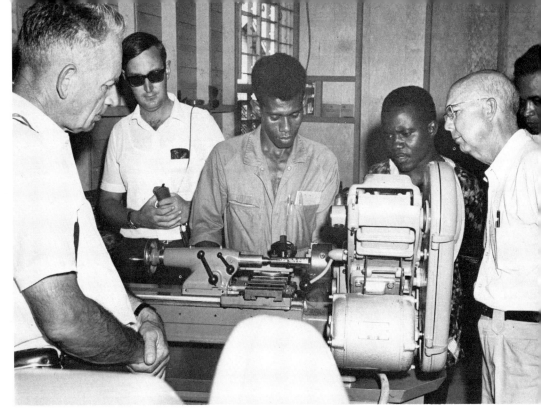

A new technical school, opened with United Nations help, will benefit some young men of Bougainville.

Australia intends to give up its control of the territory as the local people acquire the experience and education necessary for running their own affairs, and that will bring up the question of whether Bougainville should return to the Solomons or remain under the domination of New Guinea.

The Trust Territory of Australia

All of the major islands of Australia's trust territory resulted from volcanic activity. In addition to Bougainville and half of New Guinea, the main section is the Bismarck Archipelago, named for Prince Otto von Bismarck when the islands came under German rule in 1884. The archipelago, which breaks down into the Admiralty Islands, New Ireland, and New Britain, with a hundred small islands and atolls scat-

A teacher of New Ireland hopes to lead the younger generation to knowledge.

tered among the major ones, was occupied by Australians during the First World War.

Today the Bismarck Archipelago has a population of 155,000, less than one tenth of the trust territory's two million people, and covers almost 20,000 square miles of the territory's 100,000. New Britain, about half that size, ranks as another of the largest islands in Oceania. New Ireland is about a third as big, while the Admiralties have about eight hundred square miles. Perhaps 15,000 people live in the Admiralty Islands, 25,000 occupy New Ireland, and 100,000 call New Britain home.

Certain peoples of New Britain want to break away from New Guinea. Among them, the Tolai tribesmen amount to a small nation in themselves, with about 45,000 members. They have responded well to education, surpassing most other groups throughout the trust territory in becoming ready for self-government. But they hurt their cause by showing strong prejudices against other tribesmen. In the trust territory, a system of migrant labor has been worked out. Villagers are transported to plantations or mines where help is badly needed for a time and then returned home when the work slacks off. Tolai men have attacked migrants brought to their area, battling them with fists, rocks, and clubs.

Other territory people are equally violent, and most of them have responded less well to education. Many thousands lack any knowledge other than that provided by the tribe for survival. On New Guinea, the Shuamus still eat people. New Guinea also has headhunters, as do other islands, including the Solomons. After killing an enemy, these tribesmen also shrink the man's head to destroy any magic power that might have been connected with him in life.

One might wonder if an area whose people include headhunters and cannibals would ever be ready for independence. But many signs indicate that Melanesia in general is progressing. Periodically, the South Pacific Conference takes place in one of the major capitals of Oceania. Such problems as health measures, social advancement, and economic improvement come up for discussion, with Polynesian leaders usually dominating. At the fifth conference, which took place in 1962 in American Samoa, the Melanesians impressed outside observers more than they ever had before. For the first time, Melanesians appeared to be well informed on the issues discussed. Also, they had a degree of confidence that had been lacking in previous years.

Perhaps now Micronesia is the only area that needs to catch up with modern times.

Developing Micronesia

Tourists have probably seen less of Micronesia than of either Polynesia or Melanesia. Whereas the volcanic islands of the eastern and southern Pacific offer lovely waterfalls, wandering streams, exotic jungle growth, beaches of white and black sand, and varied landscapes, the northwest Pacific provides mainly one low coral atoll after another.

In Polynesia and Melanesia, the traveler can find a few cities with night clubs, cinemas, conducted tours to fascinating areas, and comfortable hotels with occasional native dancing. Micronesia has a short supply of such inviting facilities. In addition, the United States hasn't encouraged visitors to its area of Micronesia, the Trust Territory of the Pacific Islands, which isn't exactly a showplace of American achievement. Even as times change—and they must—world travelers will probably still find more to enchant them in Polynesia and Melanesia than in Micronesia.

For the geographer, Micronesia refuses to fit neatly into one section of the Pacific. The Gilbert Islands stretch across the equator. Linked with them for political reasons, the Ellice Islands fall farther south than Melanesia's Bismarck Archipelago. Among the islands above the equator, the Palau group reaches almost to Indonesia and the Marianas run north nearly to the Volcano Islands claimed by Japan. As for people, those of the Ellice Islands are Polynesian rather than Micronesian. Those of the Palaus resemble certain Filipinos, to whom they are related.

Yap boys, with two of the old stone coins behind them to the left.

Hammer DeRoburt (right), Nauru's first chief of state, admires his country's flag.

Micronesia includes more than three thousand islands, yet has only six major groups—the Ellices, Gilberts, Marshalls, Carolines, Palaus, and Marianas. A few dots of land stand alone.

Nauru Island

One island in Micronesia is of particular interest because, although it seems to be an unlikely prospect for independence, it has become the first free nation of the region. Nauru Island, covering about eight square miles, became a republic in 1968.

The population of Nauru comes to a little over six thousand people, half of whom are Nauruans. Of the other half, more than a third come from other Pacific islands, especially the Gilberts and Ellices, and a third are Chinese. The remainder come mainly from Australia and New Zealand.

A large number of outsiders live in Nauru because the island is one great lump of valuable phosphate. On the coast the soil runs up from the sea for about three hundred yards and gives the local people some farmland. But the interior is a two-hundred-foot-high deposit of phosphate, an element that is important as a fertilizer and is used in medicines. Centuries and centuries ago, where Nauru is now, the remains of sea creatures collected on a coral bed. Earth tremors then raised this area above sea level, and the phosphate rock formed from the marine organisms.

Although Germany took control of Nauru late in the nineteenth century, it was a New Zealander who discovered that the island offered wealth. In 1907 the Germans opened a mine. Australians replaced the Germans during the First World War, and after World War II the island became a United Nations trust territory under Australia.

As the mining activity increased, the Nauruans felt they must either leave or regain control of their island. They examined other islands offered them, but decided to stay and fight for their freedom. Australia and the United Nations agreed that they should have it, and January 31, 1968, became their independence day. A former schoolteacher, Hammer DeRoburt, became chief of state, and local officials, with Australian help, organized a legislative council and wrote a constitution.

As long as the phosphate lasts, the island of Nauru will be self-supporting and the people will be free of taxes, but, in 1969, De-Roburt was already in Australia conferring with the government there about what will happen to the little nation when the phosphate runs out around 1990.

The Gilbert and Ellice Island Colony

Another peak of phosphate, Ocean Island, stands about halfway between Nauru and the Gilberts. Great Britain took command of it during World War I at the request of the local people, and now it is governed as part of the Gilbert and Ellice Islands Colony. Perhaps Ocean Island will also become a free nation someday, but unfortunately, as part of a colony rather than a United Nations trust territory, it doesn't have the bargaining lever that Nauru had. Its area is smaller than three square miles, and the population comes to only three thousand people.

However, the entire colony, which is made up of the Ellices, the Gilberts, and scattered islands, is moving toward independence. Preparing for what has to come, the British are training the people for self-government. Local chiefs handle administrative duties on the village level, while European advisers stand ready to assist them. A resident commissioner heads the islands' central government, which is located on Tarawa in the Gilberts. At one time all his advisers were outsiders, but in 1970 the constitution underwent revision to arrange for a legislative council of elected members.

A subordinate administrator for the Ellice Islands has his headquarters at Funafuti, and it is uncertain whether the Ellices will stick with the Gilberts and go on being overshadowed, or seek to become a separate nation. The Ellices have been associated with the Gilberts most of the time since white men reached them.

Commodore Byron discovered the groups in 1765, and runaway European convicts and lazy beachcombers discovered them again a century later. These outsiders frequently stirred up trouble, as it gave them a chance to steal or become paid advisers when tribes fought one another. When the missionaries arrived, they tried to put a stop to all these activities, but that sometimes stirred up as much turmoil as the lawless individuals created. As a result, the local people began to distrust all white men. Christianity caught on slowly, because the islanders often proved more peaceful than some of the men who tried to force them to accept a new religion. They could not see how Christianity's actions agreed with its words.

Britain stepped in to settle the disturbances and finally gained control over the islands. She made them a protectorate in 1892. For two decades the Ellices had a separate government, but they were joined to the Gilberts during World War I.

The peoples of the two groups are generally unrelated. Those living in the Ellice Islands descend from Polynesians. The Gilbertese are

A young woman of the Gilberts.

Ellice Islanders dance a welcome
for tourists arriving at
Funafuti Airport.

shorter, darker, and more wiry, resembling the Micronesians of the Carolines.

There are only about six thousand Ellice Islanders in a total population of forty thousand, and their nine atolls consist of only 9½ square miles. The Gilberts, spread over sixteen coral islands, occupy 155 square miles. The Ellices have in the past been called the Lagoon Islands, because they have some of the most beautiful lagoons in Oceania. Living in them are such gorgeously colored fish that the region is a skin diver's paradise. As these islands become more accessible, they are sure to attract tourists interested in diving.

The Gilbert and Ellice Colony lies off the routes of international airlines, but early in the 1970's Tarawa and Funafuti became included in the schedules of Air Micronesia. Travelers can also get there by freighter. Terminals, however, lack the conveniences that tourists expect. On Tarawa, the air terminal consists of a small group of thatched roofs held up by corner poles, but since the temperature remains around eighty, there are no chill winds to make walls necessary. After the tourist arrives, he may have trouble finding a place to stay. In the late 1960's the main hotel in the Gilberts offered only two dozen rooms, but that was twice as many as the one good hotel in the Ellices could provide.

Local people find half the islands unlivable. These are in the south of the Ellice group and the north of the Gilberts. Being only a few feet above water at high tide, they flood regularly in stormy weather. That leaves about ten islands north of Funafuti and south of Tarawa on which the people can build homes, but even these livable islands lack good soil, and they have become overcrowded. As a result, British officials have talked some people into moving elsewhere, originally to the Phoenix group, but more recently to the Solomons and to Fiji.

The Marshall Islands

North and slightly west of the Gilberts, the Marshall Islands form two strings known as the Ratak (Sunrise) Chain and the Ralik (Sun-

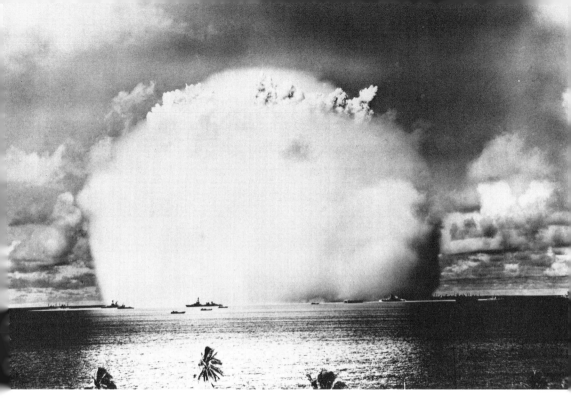

An atomic blast in Bikini Lagoon during the nuclear tests there.

set) Chain. They make up the easternmost of the six districts of the United States Trust Territory of the Pacific Islands.

Although these islands answer to the territorial government on Saipan in the Marianas, they have their own district government on Majuro in the Ratak Chain. Each of the island districts in the trust territory has a government similar to that of the Marshalls. A two-chamber house makes up the congress. The upper house consists of descendants of chiefs, but the lower house has members elected from among the people, who, in the Marshalls, number fifteen thousand. Heading the congress is a district administrator, who receives his appointment from the United States government.

In the 1960's Dwight Heine became the first man of local birth to administer the Marshalls. He is Marshallese on his mother's side, but his father, as the name suggests, came from Germany. Heine was one of

123

the first men in his district to get an advanced education. After graduating from the University of Hawaii, he rose rapidly in politics.

The thirty-four atolls of the Marshalls stretch for 700 miles across the Pacific, and have about 66 square miles of land area. The largest island of the group is Kwajalein, in the Ralik Chain. Its ninety islets have 6 square miles of land, surrounding a lagoon of 840 square miles.

Much smaller, amounting to about 5 square miles together, Bikini and Eniwetok have been separated from the trust territory. The United States wanted them for testing nuclear devices. The people on them had to be shifted to other places before the explosions could take place. Whether the tests were desirable, or even necessary, will be argued for years. Bikini had a population of about 165 people, who were uprooted and taken to Rongerik Atoll to the south. Because they proved unhappy there, officials shifted them to Kwajalein and after that to Kili. Actually, they could never be satisfied anywhere but on their home island, where they believe the spirits of their ancestors return to look after them and are unable to find them.

The United States exploded twenty-three nuclear devices on, over, or near Bikini during a period of twelve years. When the scientists miscalculated in 1954, winds carried radioactive fallout to islands outside the experimental area. Worst hit was Rongelap, about a hundred miles southeast of Bikini. Most of the population of nearly a hundred people had to be rushed to the Majuro Atoll for treatment for burns and radiation sickness, and for several years they could not return home. During that time they were kept under close medical supervision. Later, men of a Japanese fishing fleet suffered a similar accident, and the United States paid them damages. The people of Rongelap then made requests for a similar payment and eventually received about ten thousand dollars apiece.

Because of these accidents, tests on Bikini ended in 1958. The island stood deserted. Plant life sprang up once more and in tropical fashion became master of the land. By the time the United States decided the island could be returned to its original inhabitants, a jungle of underbrush covered the ground, and coconut trees, on which Bikinians depend for much of their food, had no chance to grow.

The Americans plowed up the underbrush and planted not only coconuts, but pandanus and bananas, and officially restored the island to the Bikinians in March 1970. Most of the people were not to return until the mid-1970's, but a handful came back earlier to help make the island livable again. For instance, certain crabs in the surrounding waters still contained radioactive substances, and the people had to learn what seafoods to leave alone.

At Eniwetok, the situation remained uncertain early in the 1970's. Some military officials wanted to keep it as a defense base instead of returning it to its original 150 inhabitants.

Kwajalein has already been turned into such a base. Military personnel use it to try out antimissile missiles, testing them against rockets fired from California. The people on Kwajalein receive better pay for working at the base than do Micronesians anywhere else, and observers wonder how they will be able to return to a Micronesian way of life if the base closes.

The Carolines

The Carolines stretch westward from the Marshalls for about two thousand miles. The eastern Caroline Islands are mostly coral atolls, but the western ones are a mixture of atolls and volcanic islands. They make up nearly half the trust territory's 2,140 atolls and islands, contain 460 of its 800 square miles, and have two thirds of its 100,000 people. The 960 islands have fifty different tribes, and practically every tribe has its own dialect, although, there are only half a dozen distinct languages. Of the trust territory's six districts, Ponape, Truk, Yap, and Palau belong in the Carolines. Each is a major group of islands by itself.

Ponape Island, formerly Ascension Island, with its 125 square miles, is the largest island in the trust territory and second in size in Micronesia only to Guam. Although it is situated in the coral-atoll half of the Carolines, Ponape resulted from a volcano and has a peak 2,500 feet

Hermes Katsura (right) is a Trukese who became speaker of his district's legislature. Here he is listening to District Administrator Jessie Quigley.

high, the highest in the trust territory. This mountain causes considerable moisture to fall on the island, in some years about 250 inches, a record for Micronesia and possibly for Oceania.

More interesting than its volcanic peak are Ponape's ancient ruins, Nanmatol, a city of remarkable stone structures that once must have served some ancient tribe as a capital. Modern scientists visit the ruins when weather permits, trying to learn how old they are and what the people who built them were like. A few other islands in the Carolines, such as Yap and Lele, also have prehistoric stonework.

The Truk group has fifty-five volcanic islands and forty atolls. The central ones escape many of the heavy storms that strike other parts of Micronesia. Two main tribes, once bitter enemies, occupy the group. Under European influence many of them accepted Christianity and settled down to a peaceful way of life as fishermen and farmers.

Yap is smaller than Truk, with fewer than two dozen islands and atolls of any importance. Its fame comes partly from its unusual money, which can still be found in places. Stone cutters carved great disks of aragonite from cliffs and chiseled a hole through the center of

126

each doughnut-shaped coin for a carrying pole. Two men—one at each end of the pole—could carry the smaller coins, but large ones required groups of several men. Today, fortunately, the United States dollar serves as currency throughout the trust territory.

The Palau Islands, many of which are volcanic, stand at the southwestern edge of the trust territory and of Micronesia. They make up the largest group of the Carolines, having more than two hundred islands and atolls.

The Marianas

Stretching in a five-hundred-mile chain north of the western Carolines toward Japan, the Marianas include a dozen major islands of volcanic origin, among which are Guam, Saipan, and Tinian, plus a few smaller islands and numerous atolls and reefs. The Marianas, except for Guam, which is an American possession, make up the sixth district of the United States Trust Territory, and their population numbers around ten thousand.

The Marianas have given their name to a long, deep valley on the ocean floor, which lies east and south of the islands near Guam. The valley is known as the Marianas Trench, and it reaches the greatest ocean depth known in the world—36,198 feet beneath the sea.

Life in the Trust Territory

Although its temperatures never get higher than the low eighties, the Trust Territory of the Pacific Islands suffers from earthquakes, typhoons, and stifling humidity. Yet most Micronesians would not live anywhere else. They fish their lagoons and farm their shallow soils, often with little concern for the affairs of other men. Only Micronesian peoples can own land in the trust territory. The United States leases the ground it needs from them. Sometimes, to obtain rights to a section of land, Americans have to make arrangements with an entire community or tribe.

Tribalism creates problems. Frequently one group dislikes the people of another group. In addition, each of the six districts of the trust territory considers itself superior to the other five, and where people from the different districts come in contact, fights may occur. This happens particularly around the territory's headquarters on Saipan in the Marianas, and on Yap. Workers who have come from the Palaus seeking jobs have found themselves crowded together in an area resembling a ghetto, or restricted quarter.

Most Micronesians are unskilled laborers, and many of them dislike machinery. However, with schools, military installations, and government buildings to be erected or repaired, Micronesia needs men to run bulldozers and handle other jobs in construction work. Training in construction trades has been introduced in vocational schools, but it has not been a great success. As a result, American officials have brought men from the Philippines to handle their building programs. These newcomers have received a cool welcome from the local people.

The young people of the trust territory are becoming interested in cars and in learning to drive. At the start of the 1960's, almost all the cars in the area were owned and driven by Americans. Some local men did have jeeps, which they had learned to operate during World War II and had bought after the war as Army surplus, sometimes for a dollar. Today, automobiles are more numerous, and there are traffic problems and a need for better roads. Every district leader plans to build and extend roads, but he seldom has enough money. Until the mid-1960's, most of the roads were those built in the war years and shortly after. Some of them are in such poor condition that speed limits aren't necessary. Many of the cars coming into the islands are small Japanese models, which cost less than American automobiles, but they wear out sooner than American cars on the old, rough roads.

The Micronesian Development Association

The commercial airplane is also coming to Micronesia. The Micronesian Development Association, an organization for improving and modernizing the islands, helped start Air Micronesia in the late 1960's.

With pilots mainly from the States, this airline offers schedules to major island groups. Weekly service is the rule, because Air Micronesia hasn't enough planes or passengers for daily flights on most of its routes.

A field to accommodate jets opened on Ponape in the Carolines in 1969. In 1970, the United States awarded rights to Japan Air Lines to land in the islands and made plans to do the same for Pan American World Airways. Although Air Micronesia is still too small to handle regular traffic to Japan or Hawaii, it protested. Yet the number of tourists to Micronesia increased by three fourths, to about twenty thousand, in 1970, which meant more business for Air Micronesia when these visitors had to get to islands lacking jetports. With more tourist dollars coming into Micronesia all the time, the development association has little reason to complain.

The Micronesian Development Association keeps reminding United States officials that the trust territories are supposed to become independent. Russia and Japan, through the United Nations, constantly do the same.

Efforts are being made along these lines, but they move leisurely. Voting has been introduced on the islands, with the result that some unpopular chiefs have been unseated; but elected officials often consider themselves chiefs, so democracy catches on slowly. In 1970, Micronesian officials turned down an American proposal that the trust territory receive commonwealth status similar to that of Puerto Rico. They demanded complete independence.

Governing the United States Trust Territory

Today, the United States Department of the Interior governs the trust territory through its Office of Territories. The top official in the territory receives his appointment from the President of the United States. This high commissioner is practically a president and a lawgiver combined, although a chief justice, chosen by the Secretary of the Interior, shares some of his power. A deputy high commissioner acts as an adviser to them, and in the 1960's a native of Guam became the first islander to reach this position. He was Richard F. Taitano, who was educated in the United States.

The territory has its own flag, six white stars on a field of blue. Chosen in a territory-wide contest, it went on display on United Nations Day in 1962.

A congress of Micronesia, patterned after the United States legistative body, held its first session in 1965. It can pass laws, but the high commissioner can veto them. If the congress repasses a law over his veto, he can kill it again. After that, if the congress feels strongly about it, it can submit the law to the Secretary of the Interior for final decision.

In the territory all men and women nineteen years of age or over have the right to vote. In 1965, a woman won a place in her district's government, but it hardly set off a trend. The elections since then have shown that women in Micronesia, as in all of Oceania, are far less liberated than women in the United States.

Laws of the trust territory of the Pacific Islands rest on a double standard. They are based in part on United States legal practice and in part on age-old local customs. This makes the writing of laws difficult, because customs change from one island group to another. Most judges are local men who have been trained by the chief justice, an American. They usually lack law degrees and may have little education at all. These judges not only hear cases but also decide the verdicts.

Although the chief justice introduced the jury system early in the 1960's, suitable jury members are hard to find. On any one island other than the largest, most people are related, and a defendant's relatives can't sit on his jury. Few cases involve narcotics. Those that do concern outsiders rather than local people. About the only narcotic the islanders obtain regularly is the betel (or areca) nut, which has a mild narcotic effect when chewed. Until the early 1960's, liquor was prohibited in the trust territory. Since it has been legalized, drunkenness has become a major problem.

When the United States took control of the trust territory after World War II, Micronesians respected them for being kinder than the Japanese.

Water buffalo race on Guam.

Now, however, men who feel the area should have advanced faster than it has have begun to blame the Americans. After a quarter of a century they have forgotten the cruel treatment of the past, and some of them feel they might be better off mandated to Japan, which they know has made remarkable commercial progress since the war. The more the United States debates about the territory's future, the less the Micronesians respect it. Luckily, Peace Corps members are scattered throughout the territory. As they work hard to improve living, educational, and health conditions, they are winning back the affection that has been lost by politicians and military men.

Guam

Guam fares better than the trust territory. This island of 210 square miles, which is actually part of the Marianas, has a population of fifty thousand Guamians and thirty thousand outsiders, most of them military and government personnel. The local people have American citizenship, which gives them a feeling of belonging to a nation, something Micronesians in the trust territory lack.

Although the United States President appoints their governor, Guamians do choose the members of their one-house congress. Unlike the trust territory, Guam has a number of well-educated men. Many of the professional people, such as judges and teachers, have earned degrees in local schools or in Hawaii. Although Ponape in the Carolines is growing as an educational center, Guam has long ranked as the educational heart of Micronesia.

As the United Nations promotes independence for all territories, the people of Guam will have to consider their future. Linked to Hawaii, the island might suffer the fate of an unwanted stepchild, but if it became a separate nation, it might be one of the poorest in the world. Guam will have to become more self-sufficient before it can achieve statehood in the United States. Today, the island receives considerable financial support, so many of its leaders would like it to remain a territory.

Wake and Midway Islands

Outside the trust territory, Wake and Midway lie beyond Micronesia. However, they don't lie beyond the problems facing Oceania in general.

An aerial view of Midway today.

Where are they headed? Both islands have cost the United States a lot of money, and neither has great significance except as a defense post.

Wake first became important as a station for an undersea cable from Hawaii to the Philippines. Planes later used it as a stopping-off place. Today jets bypass it. Wake still has value in an emergency, and it is a place where small planes unable to fly nonstop from Hawaii to Japan or Guam can land. It has also become a station from which space satellites can be tracked. But Wake consists of only three square miles of land, and all of its one thousand inhabitants were brought in from outside, so it will probably remain a territory.

The same holds true for Midway, even though it has a local population of some two hundred people and an area of twenty-eight square miles. Midway actually consists of two coral islands—Sand and Eastern —which stand about nine feet above the ocean's surface at high tide. Like Wake, Midway serves as a station for an undersea cable across the Pacific, and it can be used by short-range planes or those in difficulty. However, pilots making use of the landing strip at Midway must watch out for Laysan albatrosses. These "gooney birds," as the fliers call them, require a reasonably level area on which to run in order to get into the air. They find the Midway airfield quite suitable for their purpose.

When the United States decided to turn Midway into a major naval and air base, ships brought soil to cover the coral sands and make farming possible. The local residents received hogs, chickens, and cattle to supplement the large amounts of fish they ate. For the Americans who manned the various installations, attractive bushes and small trees were planted to brighten the landscape. Typically, the Americans also laid out a golf course and otherwise arranged to live in comfort.

Since Midway lies at the northwestern end of the Hawaiian archipelago, it could logically be linked with America's fiftieth state—Hawaiian monarchs in the nineteenth century did consider it part of their realm—but Midway is a military possession. It will probably remain one.

Local Life

In the 450 years since white men discovered Oceania, outsiders have influenced the islanders far more than the islanders have influenced them, and today the people of the Pacific live with a mixture of old customs and new ways, with people in or near population centers being more modern than those in villages. Yet these people have much to teach the rest of the world about living at peace with one's surroundings.

Europeans settling in the islands have generally built houses similar to those they knew at home. But even with the windows wide open, these houses can be less comfortable than the local dwellings, which are loosely built and open to breezes—and the wind is almost always blowing in Oceania. While the islanders take life easy, wear few clothes, and swim a lot, outsiders try to fight the heat with fans, cool drinks, and complaints about the climate.

Of course, outsiders who have spent many years in Oceania have learned to adjust their hours to local custom. Instead of trying to work through the middle of the day, they do most of their work before noon and after about three o'clock. A few of them have adopted native housing and dress and consider themselves to be islanders, too. This is especially true in Polynesia. People of European descent are less likely to become permanent settlers in Melanesia, except for Fiji, and Micronesia. Even those who have come to stay in Micronesia and Melanesia go elsewhere for their vacations, while the settler in Polynesia will probably spend his holidays right there.

Dressed in festival costumes, a group of villagers hope to sell their crafts to tourists.

The Caste System

An outsider who never had a servant in his home country expects to have at least one as soon as he moves to the islands. When he starts hiring a cook, maid, or yard boy, he discovers that something of a caste system exists in Oceania. The system, which is probably strongest in Micronesia and weakest in Polynesia, has helped to keep the people divided and has provided outsiders with laborers for menial and dirty jobs.

Under the caste system, certain ranks of people have little to do with certain others. In Oceania these ranks developed in various ways. Long ago many tribes had secret societies, which often handled tribal rituals. Medicine societies looked after the sick. Others had duties concerned with honoring certain spirits, or with seeking the help of spirits during a battle or a fishing expedition. In some places, such as the New Hebrides, leaders of these societies became almost as powerful as chiefs. In the same way, lesser members of the secret societies began to consider themselves above many other members of the tribe.

In Polynesia, caste more likely resulted from special abilities. A man skilled at war could fight his way to a chiefdom. His closest relatives then made up the nobility, whether they had any talent or not. Even today in many places a man descended from a chief will refuse a job as a waiter despite his need for work.

Below chiefs in rank were expert canoe builders, net weavers, spear carvers, and tool makers. At the bottom stood ordinary farmers and fishermen. However, a man who cleared more land and raised better crops than his neighbors rose above less ambitious tillers of the soil, while the fisherman who always had good luck could rise to be the leader of a fleet.

Before the Europeans arrived, the islanders did not acquire wealth. In fact, the Samoans and some others led a communistic way of life in which everyone shared whatever he had. Even a chief in Oceania had little more in the way of possessions than ordinary men. Instead, a man sought power and influence. An ambitious person helped build many canoes or planted large gardens. In that way he had more say in how the community lived.

The Ties of Kin in Oceania

Kinship has always been of great importance in Oceania, and a man has always helped his own kin first. In many places, the family line was once figured through the mother rather than through the father. A man joined the family of the woman he married, and his children paid more attention to his mother's relatives than to him. After the arrival of Europeans, this custom began to die out, and fathers in time became heads of their families. However, in Micronesia, especially away from the centers where Americans live, mother-headed households still exist.

In the past, a man shared whatever he had with his relatives. If he

The family is a closely knit unit in Oceania. This group lives in a typical Samoan house.

made a seashell scraper, he dared not refuse a cousin who wanted to borrow it. Family members would treat him like an outcast if he turned his relative away. Family pressure also worked in his favor. Unless he was disliked by his relatives, they made the borrower of his property feel like an outcast for not returning it in a reasonable length of time.

The building of a large canoe or hut required many workers. To prevent friction about who could use the completed object, the laborers were almost always very close relatives. With only one family involved, arguments seldom arose.

Because family pressures provided a system of law in Oceania, the islanders had many unfortunate dealings with white men. A European sailor might borrow an adze from an islander or accept an invitation to a feast at the local person's home. Island custom dictated that he return the tool or that he take the family a gift if he couldn't give a feast in return. But foreign sailors often kept borrowed implements and did nothing in return for favors. It took some islanders until the twentieth century to understand they couldn't deal with outsiders in the same way they dealt with family groups. Nevertheless, they remain remarkably hospitable to this day.

Islanders are conservative. All members of a family group have the same hopes, the same beliefs, the same methods of doing things. Often a man would rather cling to the outmoded ideas of his kin than gain their disfavor by changing to new ways from the outside world. This means that missionaries, educators, and other would-be helpers can produce changes only slowly.

An outsider who wants to bring about improvements in the islands needs to win a few older, respected people to his way of thinking. Through the elderly heads of family groups he can reach the rest of the population without making an obvious campaign to do so. Because the firm bond of kinship does exist, an influential older man can set off a trend, once he is convinced his championing it does not mean he is being traitorous, strange, or weak.

Everyday Life in Oceania

In families where both the mother and father take jobs, someone else cares for the children. In Tonga, for instance, grandparents generally look after them while in Western Samoa small youngsters must often look to older brothers, sisters, and close cousins for care. Missionaries hope to make parents feel more responsibility for young people.

Away from population centers, where the lack of foreigners means a lack of outside jobs, the situation is better, and old patterns exist. In remote villages, life has a set routine, as in the interior villages of Fiji. There, after a light breakfast, at times hardly more than a cup or two of tea, the men go to their garden plots or fields. They plant vegetables and harvest the ones that have matured. They also gather ripe fruits, and young men climb for coconuts. As a boy, every male learns to climb the tall coconut palms, using only his bare hands and feet. Younger children, perhaps with the aid of old people, seek firewood.

Women and girls do most of the weeding, joining the men in the gardens after caring for their housework. Since the Fijians have almost no furniture, their main household chores consist of rolling bed mats out of the way, sweeping the dirt or wood floor with a broom made of coconut fronds, and banking the cooking fire so it won't go out.

Between noon and one o'clock, work stops and the people eat the main meal of the day. Then they lie down for a nap. Toward evening, the children go swimming, while the men fish with nets or spears and the women watch or fish with hooks and lines. On islands where fishing is a major activity, the men do that in the morning and leave all the gardening to the women.

Unless incapable of work, old people in the villages have regular tasks. Besides helping to gather firewood or looking after small children, they weave mats, clean vegetables, and make tools. They may be in charge of looking after the pigs and poultry. At the same time, the elderly receive certain privileges. They can sleep longer or lie where

A flower behind the ear once carried more meaning than it does today.

the coolest breeze blows through the house. At meals, they may be served first and with the choicest bits of food. In addition, their words carry far more weight than the words of younger people.

In a gathering old people sometimes sit with their legs out in front of them. In most parts of Oceania, people sit cross-legged on the floor, and they consider it rude to have one's feet stretched out, especially if the legs point toward someone else. But an old person whose joints are stiff will be allowed to sit with his legs bent only slightly. Or perhaps he will sit sideways to the group, aiming his legs away from the other people.

What It Is Like to Be Young in the Pacific

By contrast to the old, a teen-ager must obey all rules and respect everybody older than himself. Seeing that European and American youths escape such restrictions, some young people in Oceania are torn between wanting to rebel and wanting to respect the old ways of their culture. As a result, many go abroad to seek their fortune and a freer way of life.

Few of the young people who stay remain unmarried in Oceania.

140

In the past, a girl of Polynesia indicated whether or not she was free to marry by wearing a flower in her hair. A man might do the same. A flower behind one ear meant the person should be left alone. Behind the other ear, it showed that the person would welcome companionship. Which ear depended on the custom of a particular region. The tiare, national flower of Tahiti, the frangipani, and other fragrant blossoms added to a person's allure. Today, however, this lovely custom is no longer followed, and a flower behind the ear simply means that the wearer considers it decorative.

When a boy and girl go out together in Micronesia, the boy is expected to provide betel nuts for the girl to chew. Throughout Micronesia, and most especially in Yap, the islanders chew the nut of the betel palm for its mild narcotic effect. Some people in Melanesia and Polynesia do the same, starting when they are children.

Before it is chewed, a nut is powdered all over with soft lime and wrapped in the leaf of the betel vine, which is not related to the betel palm. The juice in time turns the teeth black, and a Yapese would be embarrassed to show white teeth.

During World War II, some young men began giving their girls cigarettes instead of betel nuts. Tobacco has long been popular in Oceania. Some scientists say it was there and being chewed or smoked before white men arrived, but others doubt it.

Marriage and Morals

Before missionaries arrived in the islands, marriage customs required mutual agreements rather than binding laws. If a man and woman agreed to live together, they considered themselves married. As long as they remained happy, they stayed together, but if one or both of them became dissatisfied, they could separate. Sometimes a man might lend his wife to a close friend who was visiting from another island, but such things happened only when all parties concerned agreed. The islanders considered an act immoral only if a person was expected to do something he didn't want to do.

Island dress has changed more than housing, but costumes for special occasions often reflect the past.

Such beliefs and customs still exist in a few parts of Oceania, especially in remote areas of Micronesia. Missionaries have changed island standards considerably, but social pressures carry more weight than those of religion.

In Polynesia today, friends and family members expect a wealthy man to have a girl friend or two as well as a wife and to provide them with homes as though they were legally married to him. If he doesn't, people suspect him of being poorer than he says he is. Even his wife might prefer for him to do that, rather than have people think the family could not afford it.

Habits of Dress in Oceania

From the beginning, missionaries tried to change the islanders' habits of dress—or undress—as well as their morals. The islanders once wore little or no clothing, which is logical in a hot and humid climate, but the missionaries forced them into pants and dresses. In British colonies, where the London Missionary Society held sway over customs and costumes, clothes usually covered more of the body than in the French possessions.

However, on some islands, such as the Solomons and the Yap group, many tribes continue in their old ways even today, and loincloths and grass skirts are common. In most regions, however, shorts, slacks, shirts, skirts, blouses, and dresses have replaced them. Indian women in the Fijis often wear the traditional East Indian sari.

The most typical garment seen in Oceania, the wraparound skirt, serves men as well as women. Strings tied around the waist hold it on like an apron, except that the bindings slip through holes in the cloth so the knot can be made under the garment, where it won't show. Each region has its own name for this kiltlike apparel. Fijians call it a *sulu,* Tongans a *vala,* Samoans a *lava-lava,* New Caledonians a *manu.*

The colors preferred for these skirts vary among the island groups. In the Fijis, old people as well as young dress in bright colors. On the other hand, in the Tongas bright colors symbolize youth, so middle-aged men and women wear more gray, while older people frequently dress in black. The people of the Carolines wear brighter colors than those of the Marshalls or Marianas. Among older people on most islands, shirts and blouses are likely to be more colorful than skirts. It is commonplace for a young man to wear a skirt of gay colors and a large pattern with a shirt of different colors and a different pattern. Most of the people wear cotton clothing today, but in out-of-the-way villages, garments can still be seen that are made from the young underbark of breadfruit branches.

Because wraparound skirts are found throughout Oceania, some anthropologists assume they were being worn regularly before the arrival of Europeans. Others doubt this. If the skirt had been traditional everywhere, the doubters say, it would be worn alone. But in much of Polynesia and the more advanced parts of other islands, people usually wear it over underpants. In the more primitive areas of Melanesia and Micronesia, it is worn over a loincloth or a penis wrapper. Many anthropologists think these undergarments are the true local garb, if any was worn at all. All of them agree, though, that the wraparound skirt was known to islanders before white men came. It probably had special use in ancient times for ceremonial occasions.

Tongan men and women wear a *ta'ovala* around their waists over their skirts, pants, or shorts. This woven mat of coconut fibers may be little wider than a belt, or it may reach nearly to the ground. Older women, particularly, wear the longest ones, from armpits to ankles. In the hot, humid climate, the *ta'ovala* can be uncomfortable, which is why numerous Tongans have taken to wearing narrow ones. Many an older person considers that disgraceful. The *ta'ovala* indicates a person wants to be well dressed and to show respect to other people. Even if the garment shows ragged, worn places, people consider its wearer to be better dressed than if he had on very new, neat clothing without it. A person shows respect to friends when he wears a *ta'ovala* to their home, and he would not expect to enter a church, a courthouse, or the office of an official or a noble without it. An official might ignore a man not wearing one.

The raincoat is an important garment everywhere. Because Oceania has a rainy season, when downpours occur frequently, and a dry season, when showers come now and then, people almost always go prepared for rain. It can come on so quickly that one has no time to run home for rainwear. People with motor scooters wear their raincoats backward as a protection in front when driving through the rain. Because of strong breezes, umbrellas may prove inadequate and hard to handle, although many people carry them, too.

Except for their colorful clothing, islanders show less interest in adorning themselves than Europeans and Americans. Shark's-teeth necklaces and seashell armbands have gradually disappeared. For a festival, a person decorates himself with leaves and flowers, since they can be picked fresh anytime.

The islanders have always been proud of their thick, dark hair, and women with straight hair let it hang loose around their shoulders or down their backs. The Fijians became famous in the past for wearing their kinky hair sticking out for several inches around their heads, but during World War II, men who served in the armed forces had to cut their hair short in order to wear helmets. That led to the shorter styles that remain popular in Fiji today, especially around the capital and other major centers.

Prejudice also plays a part in keeping heads cropped short. Men of the interior continue to wear their hair in great balls, but the Europeanized Fijians consider themselves superior to the mountain dwellers and refer to them sarcastically as "big heads" because of their hair style. A man who feels this way obviously must wear his hair short to set himself apart.

Housing

Houses, like clothes, have different names according to the region and the language. The thatched hut of Fifi is a *bure*. People of the Samoas might call it a *fale*.

Before white men came to Oceania, a family lived together in a house of one room. Missionaries were shocked at this lack of privacy and tried to introduce partitions. However, in a land where fresh air is important, partitions cut off breezes and never won acceptance. Instead, some islanders hung sheets or curtains from lines, thereby dividing a house into two or three rooms while allowing air to circulate above and below the dividers.

Modern apartment houses such as this are usually occupied by foreigners rather than local people.

Basically, houses resemble one another throughout the islands. They consist simply of woven mats held up by poles, with a slanting roof of thatch to shed rain. Instead of having walls that reach from floor to roof, builders leave a space for air to flow in and out of the house. Since the roof overlaps the sides, rain cannot blow in above the walls. Generally the structure is rectangular, being longer than it is wide, although some tribes of Melanesia and Micronesia build round houses. Blackbirds taken to Australia sometimes lived in round houses there, and on their return to Melanesia began building similar huts. Where island homes have solid walls, openings for doors are left opposite each other to allow breezes to blow through. There may be a window in each end for the same purpose. Doors and windows are simply openings in poor homes. If a family wants more privacy, the mother hangs something across them.

Samoans curve the ends of their houses to form an ellipse, but they lack solid walls. A series of palm or breadfruit poles supports a roof to which woven coconut mats are attached. If a strong wind blows rain through the house, the mats can be rolled down to provide screening. At night, some of the mats may be unrolled to within a few inches of the floor to keep passersby from looking in easily. Any opening between two poles can be considered a door.

Most houses, unless built where flooding rarely occurs, have plank floors built above ground level. When the floor is high, wooden steps indicate where a person should enter and leave the building. Youngsters scramble in or jump out almost anyplace.

Throughout Oceania people commonly place houses on stilts to keep the floors dry. Buildings on low atolls have to stand above ground level, or waves will slosh through during storms.

Influenced by European structures, some islanders in major population centers build wooden frame houses. These may be of scrap lumber or other boards nailed between supporting poles, with no effort at overlapping to make the walls rainproof. A house of this sort will probably have wooden doors instead of just entrance openings, and

146

perhaps wooden flaps to cover the window openings as well. The roof may be of boards, thatch, or scrap metal.

Scrap metal for housing came into use after World War II, when the islanders salvaged parts of wrecked planes and abandoned jeeps. Away from main centers of population, people make their houses without using even nails or wire. Where pandanus grows well, it serves for thatch, as its leaves withstand rainy weather longer than coconut leaves. Dirt floors are common where flooding is no problem.

Women try to keep their cooking areas separate from the houses, except in European-type structures. This protects the families against fires and the inhalation of heavy smoke. In remote villages, the women cook over firepits dug in the ground. Nearer civilization, a woman tries to have a kitchen, preferably one built of scrap metal for fireproofing.

Most houses of the ordinary people lack bathrooms. Bathing takes place in the nearest river or at a community faucet. Only when outsiders come along and stare do people feel self-conscious about their bathing facilities. In cities, some public toilets have been constructed, but where vegetation grows as abundantly as it does in Oceania, people can easily find privacy.

Inside the house, a village family may have very little in the way of furniture. Chairs aren't necessary, since people traditionally fold their legs and sit on the floor. Only a family that invites foreigners to its home occasionally will own a few straight chairs. Floors can be covered with mats woven of coconut leaves. Such mats also take the place of beds for a great many people, although some families may stuff a cloth cover with leaves to make a mattress.

People who can afford to sometimes build or buy a bed. Yet they may continue sleeping on mats or mattresses on the floor and display the bed as a status symbol.

Baskets woven of leaves take the place of closets, dressers, and chests of drawers. Knives, forks, and spoons may be unknown in remote areas, and banana leaves can serve as plates. A few homes have wooden

Melons are popular with local people as well as with outsiders.

bowls. The closer one gets to towns and cities, the more likely one is to find the local people having furnishings similar to those of Westerners.

The Oceanic Menu

Islanders who have adopted foreign clothing, housing, and furniture still stick to the foods their forefathers knew. This pertains particularly to fruits and vegetables. They go on eating taro (also called dalo), yams, arrowroot, tapioca, *fafa* (similar to spinach), rice (especially in Micronesia), coconuts, pandanus, breadfruit, bananas, mangoes, and pineapples. Many of these vegetables and fruits were introduced from outside Oceania, but they came in long ago when the local people had little variety, and the islanders gradually grew fond of them. They don't particularly care for more recently introduced foods, such as lettuce, cabbage, carrots, tomatoes, beans, beets, custard apples, and citrus fruits.

People living on high islands have more variety in fruits and vegetables than those on low ones. Yams thrive in mountain areas, though

148

a few varieties grow on atolls. Bananas and breadfruit trees won't grow well in shallow soils.

Few plants equal the coconut in providing islanders with food. Because the nuts ripen the year round, their meat and milk are always available. The heart of the young leaf stems can also be eaten. These stem hearts are crisp, somewhat like the outer rim of cucumber slices.

Pandanus fruit resembles pineapple but must be cooked to be edible. Breadfruit also has to be cooked, either in thin slices or pounded to a paste. It tastes something like cardboard to anyone who has not been raised on it. Taro, perhaps next in importance to the coconut, also requires cooking before it can be eaten. The plant contains crystalline substances that scratch the mouth and throat like chips of glass unless the vegetable has been boiled for hours.

Inland villagers depend more heavily on vegetables and fruits than do coastal people, but some inlanders take excess crops to the shore to trade for seafood. Bonito, sharks, turtles, mammoth whales, tiny prawns, lobsters, crabs, and squid all go into the cooking pot or onto the cooking stones. While stones in a firepit accumulate heat from firewood, the housewife cleans the food and wraps it in leaves to keep it clean while it is steaming. Then she places it on the stones and covers it with dirt or mats of damp vegetation to hold the heat in.

When Europeans arrived, the islanders already had pigs, jungle fowl, dogs, and the large bats known as flying foxes to provide them with meat. The outsiders brought cattle, goats, more pigs, chickens, ducks, geese, and turkeys. European pigs proved more tender than those the islanders had brought from Asia, and they became the main course for feasts. Inland villagers of some Fiji Islands still have rules saying that a pig can be roasted only for a special occasion.

When typhoons hit the islands, food supplies may be lost. Coral atolls suffer particularly during these storms, when everything above the ground may be destroyed or swept away by the hundred-miles-an-hour winds. For months after, people may have to depend on fish to stay alive. New crops often do not grow for a year or two, until the rains have washed most of the salt left by the waves out of the soil. Once yams can be planted, they will produce food in about three months, but taro takes about five months longer than that. Coconut trees that survive a typhoon may produce again in a year or two, but where seedlings have to be planted, the people must wait seven or eight years for nuts.

Coconut milk has long been a favorite beverage among islanders. Alcoholic beverages reached the islands along with European seamen. Local peoples quickly developed a taste for them, and the problem of drunkenness has existed ever since. The French generally made liquor available to the islanders. The British more often tried to keep it from them. On an island in the New Hebrides group, the local people themselves ruled against having alcoholic beverages brought in.

Fiji has a national drink, which is known and enjoyed in the rest of Oceania as well. In Fiji the name "kava" is pronounced as if spelled *yang-GO-na,* and some writers use a spelling similar to that instead of kava. Anybody can make it, but an important person prepares it for ceremonial purposes. The bowl he uses must be of special wood, one that will not impart any flavor or ingredient to the drink. Fijians use *vesi,* a yellowish wood that turns dark brown as it ages and can stand rough handling.

The person making the kava fills the bowl with water, then crumbles and squeezes the roots of a pepper plant, also known as kava, into it. Other important men of the village sit nearby, sing or chant, and perform certain duties to "influence" the process. Kneading the roots, the host produces a drink that looks like muddy wash water, and to some outsiders tastes like it, too. One must develop a taste for kava.

The first drink of kava, served in half a coconut shell, goes to the most important man present, usually the guest of honor at the ceremony. A bearer takes it to him in both hands, for Fijians consider it rude to offer anything to another person if it is held in only one hand. Certain words are spoken by the man offering the drink and by the

The kava ceremony follows a set ritual and is a serious affair.

man accepting it. The receiver then tilts the cup and drinks it all down at once.

Kava does not make one drunk. Instead, it works as an anesthetic or tranquilizer, and the lips and mouth become numb if one drinks too much of it at one time. The islanders serve a weak version of it to tourists, the strength being adjusted by the amount of water used.

Times of Festivity and Fun

In ancient times, the islanders had few, if any, set holidays. Yet they feasted on special occasions, such as when a baby was born, a teen-ager reached puberty, a couple married, or someone died. Even the poorest groups made some effort to recognize the important moments in life. If they saw an occasion for a feast approaching, the islanders would plant extra taro and fatten more pigs. Otherwise, they made little effort to prepare for the future. They generally lived for the present. For the most part, they still do.

Family members exchanged gifts of clothing, food, animals, shell tools, and the like at ceremonial occasions, and dancing also figured in the festivities. Nothing, however, ranked in importance above eating—or does today, when guests are required to squat on folded knees for two to several hours and eat roast pig or chicken, pulling the meat apart with their bare hands.

To avoid appearing rude, a person always accepts an invitation to a banquet unless he obviously cannot attend. Even if he has been invited to two or three feasts in one day, he will insult his friend if he turns down such an invitation without an extremely good and apparent reason.

European and American festivals have given islanders new opportunities for parties. In French territories, Bastille Day is celebrated on July 14, just as in France. The local people know little about the fall of the famous prison, the Bastille, yet they hold parades, music contests, athletic events, and banquets. Festivities last at least a week in Tahiti, but in most places a one-day celebration proves enough.

In American Samoa, the people remember the raising of the American flag there on April 17, 1900. On the anniversary of that day they hold displays of dancing and singing and have sporting contests.

Western Samoans as well as American Samoans celebrate White Sunday. On the second Sunday in October, children wear white clothes to church, with garlands of white flowers wrapped around their heads. Later in the day, family banquets take place, during which adults give presents to the youngsters, for the day honors them.

During the second week in October, Fijians hold a hibiscus festival. In a carnival atmosphere, they have colorful parades that include decorated floats and marching girls. A hibiscus ball ends the week, at which time a Miss Hibiscus receives her crown.

Sporting events have mostly been imported from abroad, although islanders have long held canoe races and swimming meets. Local people now enjoy Rugby and soccer, both of which they call football, and cricket has caught on in British-held islands. Men from different

152

A tin can pulled with a string serves as a toy for these children.

island groups compete against each other in the years when the South Pacific Games take place, as on Tahiti in September 1971.

Island children, like children everywhere, have foot races, play marbles, and delight in various other amusements. A game can be made of rolling soft-drink cans down a bank to see whose can reaches the bottom first. Tiring of the game, players are likely to stomp the cans flat or throw them into the ocean, with no thought of keeping them to play with another day. Strings weighted with small sticks provide children with dueling weapons. A dueler tries to whip his string around that of his opponent and, with a sharp jerk, break the other's string, pull it out of his hand, or strip his weights off. Or a bit of driftwood or a flat leaf will make a boat that a child can push around a puddle with a stick.

In Pursuit of Knowledge, Health, and Religion

There are so many educational systems in Oceania that they could fill a book by themselves. In general, the system in any one country, colony, or island follows the pattern of the outside nation that introduced it. Differences occur because of the special needs or desires of individual island groups and also because missionaries teach according to the methods of their churches.

Almost every government in Oceania has begun to offer its children some education. Capital cities have always been the first anywhere to get government-built schools, and local people with enough education to teach in government schools usually want to remain in the capitals. As a result, missionaries have done the most about carrying education to the remote areas.

Certainly all early education in Oceania came from mission groups. Outsiders and local people alike agree that schools are one of the greatest, if not the greatest, contributions missionaries have made to the Pacific.

Elementary Schools in Oceania

Most islands are divided into districts, with each district usually having at least one elementary school. Students who live far away get

Many schools lack libraries, but the United States with United Nations help has provided good ones, like this one in Ponake, in the major schools of the Trust Territory of the Pacific.

there by public bus or by horse, or even on foot, starting as early as seven in the morning to arrive by nine. They carry their lunches. Seldom do they have books to carry, for books usually cost more than a family can afford. In many cases, the teacher is the only one who has books, and she copies out of them onto the blackboard. The children then copy down her notes so they will have something to study.

Teachers

Even after World War II, most teachers in Oceania still came from abroad. Little by little they have trained local people to take their place, although mission schools generally keep outsiders to head the teaching staff. Many local teachers lack a college education, and a third to a half will not even have finished high school. However, on Ponape in Micronesia there is a Teacher Education Center, to which instructors can go during summer vacations to complete their high-school diplomas.

Teachers fall among the poorest paid of professional people in Oceania. Unless he has at least a high-school certificate, a teacher will probably draw under a hundred dollars a month, and in some areas he will receive less than fifty dollars.

Schools in Fiji

In Fiji, the East Indians often have their own schools and prefer to send their youngsters there. The students learn Hindi, the main East Indian language in Fiji, as well as English and some Fijian. Native Fijians go to public schools, where Fijian is the language of instruction. The students also learn some English, but few Fijian educators feel they should learn Hindi. Students are supposed to go to school between the ages of six and fourteen, but many drop out.

Public education in Fiji is not entirely free, although it is in most of Oceania. The cost is about twenty dollars a year for younger students and somewhat higher for teen-agers. The school year in Fiji has three terms—February to May, May to August, and August to November

Three students may share a desk built for two, for schools are often crowded.

—with summer vacation running from November to February. Until recently, boys went to classes separately from girls. Where a school had only one room, the girls would be at the blackboard reciting while the boys remained at the back of the room doing handicrafts or studying their notebooks.

British Innovations

Teachers in British areas of the Pacific, particularly the missionaries, have worked out alphabets of local languages, which are based on the English alphabet but with variations. In many dialects of Oceania, certain letters have a double sound. For instance, *b* is pronounced as if it were the two letters *m* and *b,* and *g* sounds like *ng*. That is why names like Pago Pago turn out to sound as if spelled Pango Pango.

Another thing that British educators have done is to translate the local legends and stories that young people know from early childhood into the foreign language that they are learning. A boy learning English picks it up much more rapidly when it tells a tale he already knows.

Some schools offer sports programs, but many rely on group exercises in physical education classes.

Schools in French Polynesia

The Tahitian schools stand out among those in French areas of Oceania. Each district has an elementary school of five grades. After that come seven years of high school, which are divided into two sections, called degrees, of four years and three years each. First-degree high schools can be found in only a few major population centers of the Society Islands. At the beginning of the 1970's, second-degree high schools existed only in Papeete, where a student had a choice among three kinds—one public, one Protestant, and one Catholic. He also had to find a way to get to the capital to attend.

On entering a first-degree school, the student starts learning English (he already knows French from elementary school). Two years later he adds another foreign language, which is usually Spanish but may be German. At the start of second-degree high school, the teen-ager

158

chooses whether he wants to pursue letters and become a teacher or lawyer, or study science and become a doctor or an engineer, or learn business.

The law says students must remain in school until they are sixteen, but no one checks on dropouts. Many youngsters leave school at the end of their five elementary grades, but they cannot get jobs. All a dropout can do is help in a family business or run errands.

The highest percentage of students drop out when they reach sixteen, which is about the time most of them complete the first degree of high school. At that age they can obtain government papers that will allow them to work. Some students stop regular high school at sixteen and spend enough time in a technical or commercial school to train for a specific line of work. A trend toward attending these special schools can be observed throughout Oceania today, with almost every major island group having at least one.

Apia, Western Samoa, is rightfully proud of its modern library.

Trust Territory Schools

In 1963, English became the language of instruction in all schools of the United States Trust Territory of the Pacific Islands. Youngsters now start learning it in the first grade. A number of local people worry that the Micronesian tongues will gradually die out as English becomes the language of education, business, and government. But without a standard language of education, officials find it difficult to tell if youngsters throughout the trust territory are receiving the same quality of schooling.

No high schools existed in the trust territory before the 1960's. Today they can be found only in the six district capitals. Each high school offers some vocational training, and technical schools have been built at Truk and at Koror in the Palaus. Ponape, more centrally located than Guam, is also growing as an educational center, although Guam has the only medical school in Oceania north of Fiji.

Higher Education in Oceania

French Polynesia had no university in the past, but Tahiti has one under construction, to be completed by the mid- or late 1970's. In the meantime, any student graduating from a second-degree high school has to go to France or another foreign country for a college education.

Fiji received one of the first schools of advanced education in Oceania when the University of the South Pacific opened in Laucala, near Suva, in 1968. It attracts students from all over Oceania, but especially from Tonga and other islands where English is the main foreign tongue. Fiji also has the Central Medical School, which likewise draws young people from other regions. This school trains medical and dental technicians, but to become a full-fledged doctor or dentist, a student has to go outside Oceania. Annoyed with having to let students go to Fiji for a higher education, Tongan officials in the 1970's began asking Britain to help them build a university.

Students from families with money in English-speaking parts of Oceania often go to New Zealand, Australia, Guam, or Hawaii to attend college. Hawaii in particular proves expensive, but grants from the United Nations help some students to go abroad.

Adult Education

Throughout Oceania, adult education is generally not separated from teaching the young. If a thirty-year-old man wants to go to school, he sits in classes with students a third his age. Since English has been introduced as a requirement in trust territory schools, quite a few older Micronesians have returned to the classroom, as they recognize the value of knowing this language for business and other purposes.

Islanders who have been under one ruling nation since the arrival of whites have fared better educationally than those who have been controlled by several countries. Most adults in Tonga can read and write at least a little, but some islands of Micronesia are peopled by whole tribes who lack schooling.

In the past, a man often considered himself educated if he could add

Radio has increased educational and health programs in Nauru and all over Oceania.

161

simple sums and speak enough of a foreign language to do business with outsiders. But under foreign governments, most local peoples understood little about the laws they had to obey. In cases where tribal tradition said they could do one thing, such as take a pig from an enemy tribe, the white man's law said they couldn't. They usually followed tribal practice and landed in trouble. Seldom did a foreign lawyer come forward to assist the bewildered islander, and if he had a champion at all, it was a missionary. To avoid problems, native islanders began seeking education.

Today, especially in Polynesia, some islanders go to school to become lawyers in order to help their people. Where countries are winning independence, there must be men trained to be lawyers, government officials, teachers, doctors, and the like. What now needs to be changed in Oceania is the outdated belief that age is synonymous with wisdom and ability. Some young men doubt the sense of getting an education, because they may have forgotten much of what they have learned by the time they're respected enough to use it.

Education by Radio

Recently, some governments in Oceania have started efforts to reach outlying people by radio. The Fiji Broadcasting Commission, for example, provides educational programs in Fijian, Hindi, and English. The system works best when a teacher operates the receiving set, clarifying, if necessary, what comes over the air.

Where most of the people of an island or group of islands speak the same language, education by radio works fairly well. But in some places, such as the Bismarck Archipelago, where each tribe has its own dialect, officials wonder just how many people the broadcasts reach. Nevertheless, broadcasts were introduced in New Britain and New Ireland in the 1960's and continue to be sent out. The transistor radio makes broadcasting possible, because in most parts of Oceania only capital cities and a few other centers have electricity.

162

New Guinean and many other doctors, influenced by the World Health Organization, believe in checking for signs of trouble before illnesses actually occur.

Medical Care in the Islands

As in the case of education, most early medical care came to Oceania through missionaries. Although ships' doctors often helped the islanders when they were in port, sooner or later, they always sailed away with their vessels. Left on their own, the islanders returned to their age-old charms and chants. Missionaries, however, introduced continuing medical treatment, along with religion, and gave people a knowledge of sanitation and hygiene.

The most serious diseases of the past were malaria (including black-water fever), leprosy, yaws, filariasis, hookworm, tuberculosis, dengue fever, and elephantiasis. Coastal and low-lying areas in particular suffered from diseases carried by the mosquito, such as malaria, dengue, and elephantiasis. The Second World War brought about many campaigns to fight these diseases, because troops arriving in the South Pacific faced as much danger from disease as they did from the enemy. As a result, Allied health officers launched programs to wipe out malaria and various other ailments.

These Samoan technicians may have to perform the duties of doctors or nurses at times. The United Nations has helped them get their training.

After the war, local governments made major efforts to improve the health standards of their countries, yet today the people suffer from internal parasites and malnutrition as well as from tropical diseases. Some doctors automatically try to rid their young patients of worms twice a year, taking it for granted they will have picked up parasites from dirt or poorly cooked food.

Many a person in Oceania who calls himself a doctor has had only two or three years of medical training. Usually, he has been educated to be a technician in a clinic or hospital, but because remote islands need doctors, the authorities are forced to send him there to carry on the work of a fully educated physician.

Some islands, such as the New Hebrides, have nurses who walk from village to village to aid people where there are no doctors. The World Health Organization helps train them.

Thanks to short-wave radio, these medical technicians seldom have to rely entirely on their own judgment. Faced with a problem beyond their knowledge or abilities, they can radio to a district hospital for advice. The airplane also helps them. In an emergency, they radio for a doctor to fly to their assistance or send for an ambulance plane to carry a patient to a hospital.

Hospital Facilities in Oceania

New hospitals are being constructed regularly throughout Oceania. Every capital has one, and most governments now hope to provide one for every district. Each district of the trust territory in Micronesia already has at least one, supposedly headed by an American doctor, but there are periods when an American may not be on hand.

The Central Medical School, in Fiji, trains technicians from many parts of Oceania.

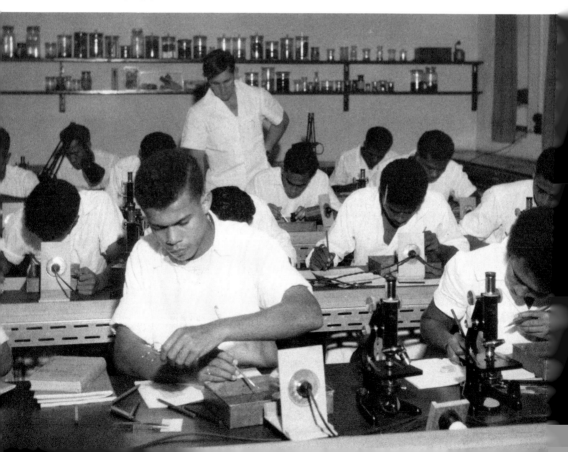

Finding physicians willing to give up profitable practices in the United States to go to the islands proves difficult. The situation is similar throughout Oceania. Only in places where doctors can have some private practice as well as hospital work are fully educated men willing to spend a few years. They make their money privately treating outsiders, who prefer to avoid the crowded and sometimes uncomfortable conditions of local hospitals.

Western Samoa has no doctors at all in private practice. Almost all medical service is provided at clinics without charge.

Tonga completed a new hospital in Nukualofa in 1970, although most of it didn't open until the next year. A number of its doctors and pharmacists come from other places. Especially numerous are New Zealanders, sent by their Volunteer Service Abroad, which resembles the United States Peace Corps. The Peace Corps also sends a doctor and some helpers to Tonga.

Unfortunately, almost all public hospitals in Oceania have a scarcity of equipment, trained personnel, and medicine. Often missionary clinics are better equipped.

Superstition and Medicine

In treating their patients, doctors must use care in handing out drugs. Islanders often assume that a medicine that is good for one ailment will also be of use in combating another. When medical men introduced quinine tablets to fight malaria, some islanders took them as substitutes for aspirin in cases of headache.

Doctors must also struggle against superstition. A man may believe that a strand of his hair, a broken piece of fingernail, or a waste product can be used against him by his enemies in a magic ritual that will kill him or at least make him ill. Consequently, when a doctor needs a sample of blood or urine, a highly superstitious person will refuse to let him have it. That can make a doctor's life difficult, but such a belief does serve a useful purpose as far as sanitation is con-

Education and religion are closely linked, and mission schools like this one are among the most attractive in many parts of Oceania.

cerned. People bury their wastes or otherwise dispose of them so that they never become a village nuisance.

Early Religious Belief

Some islanders who go to a Christian church still worry secretly about spirits that just might exist in streams, trees, or rocks, and they suspect that typhoons and other natural disasters have been sent by these spirits to punish them for being wicked.

The early islanders generally believed in two classes of spirits. Certain ones had always been supernatural beings—the creator and his helpers. There were others who had started out as human beings—usually chiefs or religious leaders—but who had performed what the people took to be miraculous deeds. The people assumed that these leaders became members of the spirit world after they departed from their earthly bodies.

To this day, ancestor worship remains strong in Micronesia, even among people who attend Christian churches. Many Micronesians believe that there is a spirit living in every person's head and that it escapes when he dies. For four days this spirit hovers around the dead person's grave, but in time it usually departs. Sometimes, however, a spirit makes it known to the people that it is still in the area. Through some person chosen as a spokesman, the spirit predicts coming events. If the spokesman's forecasts frequently prove accurate, his fellow villagers believe he speaks for a "great ghost." Such a spirit ranks above all the "little ghosts," which hold favor for only a few weeks or months. Missionaries naturally say that such spirits don't really exist, but they have never been able to explain to everyone's satisfaction why some predictions come true.

Missionaries—For and Against

The Fijians have a Pocahontas-type story about a missionary and a beautiful island girl, dating from the days of cannibalism. When her tribe was about to toss the unfortunate minister into a cooking pot, a chief's daughter rushed forward and begged that he be allowed to become her husband. The missionary preferred marriage to being eaten, and as far as anybody knows "they lived happily ever after."

Apparently later missionaries didn't try to make the Fijians give up this tale, but from the very beginning, church representatives attempted to force islanders to give up some of their ways of life. For instance, James Wilson of the London Missionary Society was horrified at island dancing. True, some dances did represent sexual acts, but Wilson banned *all* dances, and the same thing happened under other missionaries throughout Oceania. Fortunately, various dances have been preserved because the people continued to practice them in secret. If they had done otherwise, the world might have lost one of the genuine art forms of Oceania.

As well as dancing, the people of Oceania delight in anything musical. The lovely hymns and musical rituals of the Christian churches appealed strongly to them. The Methodism of the London Missionary Society caught on rapidly, in part because it included much hymn singing. Because all the vowels, which are numerous in Oceanic languages, have to be sounded, the hymns underwent revision. Outsiders have trouble recognizing familiar melodies because many notes have been added to take care of the vowels, and other notes have been decreased in value to allow the extra ones to fit in.

However, hymns, Bible teaching, medicines, and schools all failed to attract islanders to Christianity in a number of places. Where

As they sing, recite, or take notes, youngsters find that keeping cool rather than warm is the problem in most schools in Oceania.

measles and smallpox broke out after the arrival of missionaries, the islanders found it difficult to believe the epidemics could come from the followers of a peaceful, forgiving, or loving God. They wanted nothing to do with men who offered killing sicknesses along with their religion.

Conflicts between different mission groups also turned some islanders away. In the Solomons, Seventh-Day Adventists and Methodists burned down each other's churches. Neither side benefited, for they left the people doubting that a Christian God existed. Yet rivalries—often more political than religious—continued up to the time of the Second World War.

On occasion, missionaries have brought about political improvements. That happened in Tonga, where wars killed so many men that females always outnumbered males. King Taufa'ahau, who gained the throne in 1845, sought a way to end the repeated conflicts, and Wesleyan missionaries convinced him that Christianity was the answer. After the king accepted the Christian religion, the people followed his lead and today all Tongans are Christians.

King Taufa'ahau gave up his pagan name and ruled under the name of George Tupou I. When he suspected that officials of the church, mostly living in Australia, were draining off the local contributions for use elsewhere, he demanded an accounting. Shirley Baker, a missionary, supported the king and was dismissed from the church as a result. The king then made Baker prime minister and with him founded the Free Church, often referred to as the Methodist Church of Tonga. Baker carried much weight; he convinced the king that the country could be ruled more wisely through a legislature. Tupou I surrendered his absolute powers in 1862 and allowed a constitutional monarchy to develop.

The Church Today

Ever since the time of Baker and Tupou I, the state and church in Tonga have been closely linked. The church got the legislature to

The Mormon churches of Oceania all resemble this one.

pass a law forbidding people to do anything of a nonreligious nature on Sundays. In the second quarter of the twentieth century, people gradually forgot about the law, and for many years after World War II it was almost completely ignored. Sunday ball games became common occurrences. During the 1960's, businessmen wanted to remain open on Sundays, but church officials reminded them of the old law. The businessmen decided to fight back. They prompted law-enforcement officers to raid Sunday parties and soccer games in the hope that such nuisance interference would get the legislators to change the old statute. So far they have not succeeded.

The Catholic Church is strongest in French-dominated areas. Otherwise, the Methodist Church holds the most power in Oceania. The Methodist congregations of the South Pacific are under the direction of the Methodist Church of Australia, which has its headquarters in Sydney. That includes the church of Tonga, which found it difficult to operate as a separate religious organization.

In 1970, the Reverend C. Kingston Daws, president-general of the Methodist Church, visited various island groups under his jurisdiction. The church is active in helping its people to better their living conditions. For instance, on Tonga, Daws talked with the people about starting beef and copra industries there to help support members of the congregations.

A relative newcomer to Oceania, the Mormon Church, or the Church of Jesus Christ of Latter-day Saints, works hard to win converts. Whereas most Protestant and Catholic church groups seek to bring Christianity to those men who still hold pagan beliefs, the Mormons try to convert other Christians as well as pagans.

Tales in Movements, Words, and Wood

Dancing as a Way of Life

Outsiders who know nothing of island dancing call all the dances of the South Pacific the hula. Only one dance should go by that name, and it comes from Hawaii, although it is danced in other parts of Polynesia. In the true Hawaiian hula, the dancer uses mainly his hands and arms. Other dances make use of other parts of the body.

A dance seen frequently in programs of local talent is the *tamure,* or *tumare,* as it is called in Tahiti. In this dance, the performer hardly moves the upper body at all, but makes expressive use of the hips and legs. The *paoa* of Tahiti requires rapid foot movements, perhaps even stomping of the feet, while the *siva,* a Samoan dance, involves more swaying. The *siva* used to be done by girls whose bodies had been greased with coconut oil until they glistened in the moonlight.

All dances originally told stories, particularly about the long canoe trips made by ancient navigators. The little genuine dancing that is still being done today continues to relate these age-old legends. Authentic dancing proves quite difficult, however, and performers now often simplify the movements. In addition, they have learned that tourists find amusement or excitement in movements that had no place in the original dances. So the performers add flourishes to win the favor of their audiences.

A girl of the Society Islands demonstrates a dance, while companions wait their turns.

Dancers of Yap prepare to perform a dance called the *mit-mit* for United Nations officials.

Major hotels throughout Oceania try to have dance programs to entertain their customers. As a result, dancing has become a way for especially talented islanders to make a living, whereas it used to be a part of sacred or warlike ceremonies. The important thing today is to attract crowds to the hotel, so that the manager will feel the venture has been profitable. When he does, he'll have the performers return at least once a week. Whenever a cruise ship spends a few days in port, a hotel may offer extra nights of entertainment.

A good dance program also attracts islanders and resident foreigners. There is hardly anyone in the South Pacific who doesn't enjoy the local dancing. An outsider generally doesn't know what parts of a dance are authentic, but he can tell by observing the local people in the audience. They usually laugh or joke among themselves when a dancer or group throws in commercialized touches. Whether they perform professionally or not, most islanders know how the dances should be done. They start learning them at about the age of four.

Before the arrival of white men, male drummers accompanied the dancers. If they desired music while they danced, both men and women might chant or sing. For instance, the *hivinau* and the *aparima* of Polynesia included both singing and dancing. The words accompanying a dance might tell the same parts of a legend that the movements expressed, or they could give additional meaning to the tale.

The guitar is now used sometimes as an instrument of accompaniment to a dance, but it was unknown before the arrival of white men. An instrument of Portugal, the ukulele, came to the islands after the

War dances, such as this one once performed by Fijian cannibals, are for men only.

mid-1800's. It never gained the popularity in other islands that it did in Hawaii, and it can be considered a symbol of catering to tourists.

In the past, working people had songs that gave them pleasure or rhythm while they labored. These—such as the *himene tarava* of fishermen, which accompanied the launching of a boat, rowing, or casting nets—had no dance. The physical motions of doing the task at hand took its place.

The Lore of the Storyteller

Islanders told legends in words as well as through dances. Parents and storytellers handed them down to children, and some of the same ones can be found in all three sections of Oceania. Because each storyteller adds his own touches to a tale, a legend may vary from one island to another, and a character can have several names, a different one for each region in which his story is told.

A favorite folktale hero is Taga, who might be called the Paul Bunyan of the islands, especially of Micronesia. Like Bunyan, he was a giant who performed remarkable deeds that suited a man of his size and strength. Iolofath, a practical joker or trickster, takes the leading role in a number of different legends. A character might also not have a name at all. The central figure in the following Melanesian story has none, at least not on some of the islands where his tale can be heard.

A young cannibal got into trouble on his home island. Fearing his people would eat him as a punishment, he slipped away from his guards after dark and swam out to sea. After a night of swimming, he reached another island, where no man lived. There he thought he would be happy, but he soon grew hungry and thirsty. He found some shellfish to help satisfy his hunger, but nowhere could he find a drop of fresh water to drink. At that point he thought it might be better to swim back to his home island, where his people would put him to death quickly. On this deserted island he would slowly die of thirst, a much worse punishment. As he thought of going home to be eaten, tears flowed from his eyes.

Suddenly a voice asked why he cried. It was a spirit that spoke, and it listened to his story with interest. When he finished, the spirit told him to take from the beach a rock the size of his head and bury it where his tears had fallen. The next morning he would find a tree had grown from it, from which would dangle similar rocks. He should climb the tree and drop one of the rocks to knock off its outer covering. Then he should crack it open with a stone, being careful to lose nothing that was inside.

The young man thought this sounded crazy, but his only other choices were to die a slow death or go home and die a quick one, so he found a rock on the beach and planted it where his tears had moistened the ground.

Night had come, so he lay down nearby to sleep. When he awoke, a tall tree stood where he had planted the rock. Because of its rough bark, he could climb it without slipping. He picked one of the round objects growing under big leaves at the top, and when he dropped it to the ground, the object's outer husk split off. Carefully he broke the inner part with a stone and found inside a delicious white liquid and white meat.

Saved, he lived a long and happy life on the island. After he died, the fruit of the tree produced other trees, which spread over the island. Some floated to other islands and in time reached all the South Pacific. Today the fruit of this tree is known as the coconut.

Other tales have less happy endings. One tells about a rat that had an encounter with an octopus. This legend in varied forms occurs among tribes of both Melanesia and Polynesia and is probably known in Micronesia as well.

A rat annoyed his shipmates by being late when they wanted to set sail from an island on which they had been gathering food, so they left without him. When the rat discovered he had been left behind, he began to weep. An octopus rose from the water and asked why he was so sad. After hearing his story, the octopus agreed to take him to his home island.

The rat rode on the head of the octopus, which, swimming with eight legs, made great speed. Soon the rat saw his homeland in the distance and felt happy. For the first time he took a good look at the creature that was carrying him and saw how unattractive the octopus was.

As soon as the rat safely set foot on his island, he began to laugh at the octopus for being ugly. He even threw seeds at the octopus, and they stuck to the eight legs and formed sucking disks along them. The octopus' friendship turned to hatred. He threw a stick at the rat, which hit him in the backside and became a tail.

Since then, fishermen who want to catch an octopus take a seashell and a coconut leaf and make a figure out of them to resemble a rat. Any octopus that sees this object dangling in the water will grab it in anger and won't let go, thereby allowing himself to be pulled ashore or into a fisherman's boat.

Such a legend hardly sounds like a Christmas story, yet in Tonga today you can buy a Christmas card with a scene on it to represent the tale of the octopus and the rat.

Island Handicrafts

Ancient crafts and artwork had a practical purpose in the eyes of the makers. When the people made utensils of carved wood or polished seashells, they created objects to be used in the course of living. Gorgeous cloaks of feathers or decorations of shells served to set chiefs, priests, and nobles apart from lesser-ranking people. Islanders created beautifully woven mats and handsomely carved temple poles to honor the spirits.

Wood-carvers can be found in almost all the island groups today, and each artist prefers his work to that of another tribe or another island. Outsiders have been especially impressed by the carvings done by men of the Gilberts, Tongas, Marquesas, and Pitcairn.

Although many Melanesian and Polynesian men continue to carve, Micronesians in the trust territory do little woodworking. Once the Palauans did especially handsome work, but they became discouraged under the Germans and Japanese. Micronesian men used to build clubhouses on the roof supports of which artists painted and carved scenes from a village's history. The Germans tore down these clubs and shipped the beams and rafters to museums of primitive art in Europe. Under the Japanese, most men had too much hard labor to perform to have free time and energy for carving or painting.

The Americans have since tried to encourage clubhouse art, but the local people have yet to regain their former interest in it. Tattooing, once a major art form in various parts of Oceania, has also lost popularity.

Palauan artists tell legends on a series of shingles, called story boards. On these thin boards they tell their tale by carving or drawing pictures, or they may combine carving and painting. It might sound as if these boards were done for children, but they most definitely are not. The stories told involve adults in adult activities, and anybody younger than a teen-ager usually gets no chance to see them.

Unfortunately, a Palauan artist can hardly make a living by painting or carving, and the same holds true throughout most of Oceania. Talented men turn their efforts toward decorating shops and painting windows with illustrations of the merchandise to be found inside. When that isn't enough to keep their families alive, they make posters, paint signs, and perhaps even paint a European-style house.

Micronesians produce some handicrafts for tourists, and will do more of this sort of work as the flow of visitors increases. But they will probably always lag behind the busy Melanesians and Polynesians, who weave and sew and pound to turn out attractive handbags, floor mats, clothing, sandals, baskets, and other souvenirs.

Simple designs rather than stories decorate woven handcrafts.

Many islanders in Polynesia and Melanesia and a few in Micronesia make *tapa* cloth, a truly local product. The people take the inner bark of paper mulberry, or *tapu,* trees and put it to soak. After it softens, the women pound it over and over until a mass of it fuses together to form one large thin sheet of sand-colored cloth, twenty or more feet long and twelve or more feet wide.

It takes several days to a few weeks to make a length of *tapa,* depending on how regularly the people work at it and how many of them take part. One person alone doesn't produce it. Usually a few families, often related to one another, work together. The cloth will generally be sold by the family that owned the *tapu* trees from which the bark came, but the members of that family are obligated to assist the other families in turn.

182

Designs on the cloth, usually in black or brown from plant juices, or sometimes from commercial dye, represent a variety of scenes or objects. Perhaps they tell an island legend, depicting the island as a mound with two or three treelike appendages. In Tonga, people use patterns to represent Queen Salote's necklace and tiara even though she died in the 1960's. Words, perhaps of greeting or possibly a wish of good fortune, may be included, too.

If a member of a family has become friendly with an outsider, the foreigner will not be asked to pay for a piece of *tapa* cloth. A gift of money in exchange for it may be graciously accepted, but no sign will indicate to the outsider whether he has been stingy or generous. He will be left with the feeling that his friendship is the important thing.

The women of many families also weave various articles for sale, with each family claiming that its work and designs are exclusive with it. Yet when you see a large market set up on the days a cruise ship is in port, you will discover overlapping designs and workmanship. If you pointed this out to a proud workman—and they're all proud, usually with good reason—she would laugh good-naturedly. Secretly she would consider you to be short on manners.

Artists from the Outside

Many outsiders of talent have been attracted to the South Pacific. One of the best known was Paul Gauguin, the French painter who left his family in Europe to live among the islanders of Polynesia in the 1890's. His pictures of native women are recognized throughout the world.

On Tahiti, you may hear it said that the local people hate Gauguin because he introduced venereal diseases there, but, whatever he did to anger the islanders, he cannot be accused of that. Captain Cook's journals show that a fourth to a third of his men became diseased in Tahiti, so the sailors of Bougainville and Wallis probably introduced venereal troubles more than a century before Gauguin arrived. The French artist can only be accused of drinking too much and making

Ia Orana Maria by Paul Gauguin.

A handsome museum on Tahiti stands as a memorial to Gauguin, but it contains only copies of his works. The originals are all in noted galleries around the world.

IA ORANA MARIA

a nuisance of himself at times, but he also produced handsome works that have helped attract visitors to the South Pacific.

John La Farge painted in the Samoas and other parts of Polynesia on a trip of several months that he took there in 1890. However, he apparently escaped catching "island fever," for he returned to his family in New England.

Following in Gauguin's footsteps in more recent times came Edgar Leeteg, who lived on Moorea and died there in 1953. His specialty was painting Tahitian women on pieces of black velvet. For a time he had difficulty reaching a market, but today you cannot find an owner of one of his pictures who will part with it. Other artists making names for themselves in Oceania are Serge Gres from Russia and Adrien Herman Gouwe from the Netherlands.

Writers from the West

Pierre Loti helped make the world aware of Oceania through writing. A sailor who spent much time in the Pacific, he met a lovely Tahitian girl with whom he fell in love. Instead of calling him by his real name, Louis Marie Julien Viaud, she nicknamed him Pierre Loti. When he began writing novels and travel books, he used that name. His *Rarahu*, published in 1880 and later retitled *Le mariage de Loti*, told of his happy life on Tahiti. Much of Loti's writing shows strains of melancholy and pessimism, but the passages describing his association with the Tahitian girl have lyric charm.

Herman Melville, best known for *Moby Dick*, also reached the South Pacific as a sailor. Dissatisfied with life on a whaler, he deserted the ship in the Marquesas. For months he lived among cannibals, an experience he later turned into the book *Typee*. Escaping on another whaler, he reached Tahiti, only to be jailed because of his part in a minor mutiny. These adventures and others that followed also led to a book—*Omoo*—which gives a picture of life observed and lived by sailors in Polynesia. One chapter describes a moonlit dance unlike anything you can see in Oceania today.

Robert Louis Stevenson posed with his Samoan servant at his home in Western Samoa.

We waited impatiently; and, at last, they came forth. They were arrayed in short tunics of white tappa; with garlands of flowers on their heads. . . .In an instant, two of them, taller than their companions, were standing, side by side, in the middle of a ring formed by the clasped hands of the rest. This movement was made in perfect silence.

Presently the two girls join hands overhead; and, crying out, "Ahloo! ahloo!" wave them to and fro. Upon which the ring begins to circle slowly; the dancers moving sideways, with their arms a little drooping. Soon they quicken their pace; and, at last, fly round and round; bosoms heaving, hair streaming, flowers dropping, and every sparkling eye circling in what seemed a line of light.

Melville's descriptions have kept people reading *Omoo* for over a century and a quarter.

Best-loved among writers from outside, Robert Louis Stevenson spent his last years in the Samoas. Often dressing like a penniless, sloppy beachcomber, he joined the local people in cutting trees and doing menial tasks. He also took an active part in politics, always siding with the islanders against the encroachments of foreigners. The people loved him for his storytelling ability as well as for his sincere helpfulness. They called him Tusitala—Teller of Tales. When he died in 1894, at his home a few miles outside Apia, they carried his body high up Mount Vaea and buried him in a special tomb. Both the house and tomb are tourist attractions today, but to many local people they are more like sacred shrines.

Stevenson's *The Beach of Falesá* takes place in the South Pacific. A short novel written during the author's Samoan years, it tells of the love between an Englishman and a local girl. While unwinding the plot, Stevenson gave brief, fascinating glimpses of island life and scenes.

> On we went, in the strong sun and the cool shadow, liking both; and all the children in the town came trotting after with their shaven heads and their brown bodies, and raising a thin kind of a cheer in our wake, like crowing poultry.

> The light of the lantern, striking among all these trunks and forked branches and twisted rope-ends of lianas, made the whole place . . . a kind of a puzzle of turning shadows. They came to meet you, solid and quick like giants, and then spun off and vanished; they hove up over your head like clubs, and flew away into the night like birds. The floor of the bush glimmered with dead wood. . . . Big, cold drops fell on me from the branches overhead like sweat. There was no wind to mention; only a little icy breath of a land breeze that stirred nothing; and the harps were silent.

A team of storytellers who devoted many novels to the South Pacific were Charles Nordhoff and James Norman Hall. Nordhoff, from California, and Hall, of Iowa, met in France during World War I when they both served in the Lafayette Escadrille, a famed flying corps. Their history of the Escadrille, published in 1920, attracted the attention of a leading American magazine, which gave them an assignment in the South Seas. This led to twenty-five years of collaboration, although each of them also published books on his own. Nordhoff, for example, wrote *The Pearl Lagoon* especially for young readers.

A true South Pacific adventure captured the attention of Nordhoff and Hall and led to the three books that brought them their greatest fame. The first one, which appeared in 1932 under the title *Mutiny on the Bounty,* told the story of Fletcher Christian's uprising. Two years later the second novel, *Men Against the Sea,* chronicled Captain Bligh's remarkable voyage across the Pacific after being set adrift. *Pitcairn's Island,* also published in 1934, dealt with the lives of the mutineers until they settled on a final home.

Perhaps Nordhoff and Hall would have written of Paul Gauguin's life in Tahiti had not another novelist beat them to it. W. Somerset Maugham published *The Moon and Sixpence* in 1919, picturing Gauguin, under the name Charles Strickland, as a romantic rebel.

Maugham knew the locale of which he wrote, for he had traveled in the Pacific. At Pago Pago, you can still see the building in which he stayed while visiting American Samoa. A young woman from his ship also reportedly stayed there, and perhaps she was the model for the central character in Maugham's short story "Miss Thompson." The tale gives a good indication of what it is like to undergo day after day of rain during the wet season in Oceania. When John Colton and Clemence Randolph turned the story into the successful play *Rain,* Sadie Thompson became one of literature's famous characters.

A lighter, frequently gayer picture of the islands can be found in *Tales of the South Pacific* by James Michener. Stationed in the Pacific during World War II, Michener published the work in 1947 and received a Pulitzer Prize for it. When Richard Rodgers, Oscar Hammerstein II, and Joshua Logan turned it into the musical comedy *South Pacific,* its interlocking stories reached a wide audience in the theater and on the motion-picture screen. But you need to read the book to get a picture of Oceania as a place rather than as an arena for the activities of interesting characters. Less successful but interesting for beautiful Pacific scenes is Cinerama's *South Seas Adventure* film.

Entertainment in the Islands

Television arrived in Oceania during the 1960's. Among the first islands to receive it, Tahiti began broadcasting in 1967. A few programs of local interest originate in Papeete, but most come from France. French is dubbed into all programs that originate in other languages.

Watching television programs and going to movies are among the most popular entertainments with Tahitian teen-agers. About the only activity that ranks above them is dancing, although beach activities, soccer, and fishing also fill up much of the free time of young people.

Most localities of Oceania lack theaters. When a play does get a local production, it will be presented in a school or at a cinema. Little original work is being written in the islands, but a high-school teacher interested in drama may encourage students to write skits.

When they can, local people attend plays, especially musicals, and occasionally a touring company comes from Europe, particularly to French Polynesia. Tahiti may get a troupe from France once or twice a year, presenting modern versions of the old theater classics by Molière and Corneille. As a result, one theater for plays operates in Papeete, but it is not a business that could be classed as a major one in Oceania.

Surviving in Oceania

Islanders of Oceania have always had the reputation with outsiders for being lazy, but most of them can work hard for long hours if necessary. In a region where nature provides them with crops for little effort, why should they tire themselves to acquire things they don't really need?

Money has not yet become important to the average islander, who values personal freedom above wealth. If a man's income satisfies his daily needs, he frequently makes no effort to earn more. As a result, the owners of factories, plantations, or stores find it difficult to increase their output or improve the efficiency of their businesses. Many times it does no good to offer a raise or bonus to an islander when it exceeds what a man thinks he requires. Instead of encouraging a worker to try harder, a raise often encourages him to take a day off to rest or fish. Even people who live on the verge of starvation some of the time prefer free time to money.

When the Europeans arrived in New Caledonia, they found the people farming with stone tools. When crops proved poor, the tribesmen struggled to survive. The outsiders introduced metal agricultural implements, so that a man could clear more land in a day's time and his wife could turn more soil and plant more seeds. Instead of increasing production, however, the people grew the same amounts as before—

A worker scoops the meat from the coconut shell at a copra plant.

enough to satisfy their day-to-day desires. What they had gained was more time for leisure.

Land Ownership

Partly because people left acres lying idle, but more because of greed, outsiders often won control of the land in Oceania. They did it by four main methods.

In the most honest way, an individual purchased a farm directly from a tribe or a family so that buyer and seller usually knew exactly what land was involved. A second method saw the government of an island group buying productive tracts of land. In that case, where islanders failed to understand foreign terms such as "acres" and "square miles," they could be badly shortchanged. The government might then sell the land to individual outsiders for far more than the purchase price.

An even less ethical practice was for some government to claim all land lying idle, paying the local people nothing for it. But, worst of all, some governments took control, by force, if necessary, of all land, whether it lay idle or not. The Polynesians resisted these efforts to take their lands better than the Melanesians and Micronesians did. As a result, Tongans, Tahitians, and Western Samoans still own much of the soil of their islands, and there are even laws to keep them from selling it to outsiders.

A century ago, Tonga's system of land distribution appeared to be the wisest in Oceania. The government decreed that every young man, on reaching the age of sixteen, would receive about eight acres of land in the country for farming and a small plot in a nearby town for building a home. During the first year of ownership, he had to plant two hundred coconut trees, and after he married, he had to raise enough vegetables to feed his family. This system worked well until the 1960's, when all the usable land was gone.

Perhaps today if young men would agree to go to remote islands they could still have some land, but more and more of them want to

192

settle on Tongatapu. About seven thousand teen-agers in the Tongas remained landless in 1971, and the number increases every year.

Because of the landownership system, you seldom see fruit and vegetable markets in Tonga. Those you do find are small. Some islands, such as Tahiti and the main one of Fiji, have large covered areas where people display garden and orchard produce. But since most Tongans still have land and are supposed to be able to raise their own fruits and vegetables, markets have little place as yet. Only foreigners and the operators of restaurants and hotels need to seek out stalls at which to purchase garden foods. The big markets of Tonga are usually fish markets in coastal settlements.

Agriculture on the Islands

Missionaries, Peace Corps workers, and some governments have all tried to educate the islanders in better agricultural methods. Their efforts have been less successful than officials hoped they would be. Most islanders have little hope of owning tractors, plows, or other implements necessary for modern farming. In addition, some of them realize they are learning practices that are more useful on large acreages than on the small plots owned by so many people in Oceania.

After returning to their villages, numerous agricultural students take up the old ways of their parents. That is partly because women do much of the farm work in remote areas. If a young man from such a community returned from school and helped the women, he would be scorned.

Agricultural experiment stations have been set up in various parts of Oceania. Outsiders generally run these stations, with the aid of local assistants. Their purpose is to develop disease-resistant vegetables and to find new ones that can thrive in the islands. Coral atolls need more fruits and vegetables that will grow in poor, thin soils.

The scientists also seek ways to fight cacao-tree borers and rhinoceros beetles. One fortunate thing about the great distances between islands

New Britain farmers learn about cacao trees at an experimental station, which the United Nations has helped start.

is that vegetation blights spread slowly. Estimates say half the coconut trees of the Palaus have been destroyed by the rhinoceros beetle, which ruins the blossoms, but the Marshalls are free of this insect pest. A breadfruit disease on Pingelap, in Micronesia, has been confined to that island.

The king of Tonga takes a personal hand in improving crop production in his islands by encouraging agricultural fairs. More than that, during August and September every year, he visits the various islands and communities of his domain when they hold their farm shows. He and the royal family travel all over the kingdom to attend every fair they possibly can. People make an effort to produce good crops to exhibit when he comes.

Many islands produce identical crops. Throughout Oceania, taro and coconuts have special importance because they grow under poor conditions. Low islands frequently have a central area lower than the rim. Since taro needs a swampy place in which to grow, the people often use this low central section of an island for taro gardens.

Next to taro and coconuts, major crops of the islands include yams, breadfruit, bananas, pandanus, and sugarcane. Farmers and gardeners also grow melons, pineapples, ivory nuts, oranges, peaches, apples, grapes, corn, vanilla, coffee, and tobacco. Except for growing taro, the best gardens can be found on gentle mountain slopes and on plateaus that aren't too high. Ancient lava beds have generally turned into good soil, with good drainage, and there are no settlements on them to take up most of the ground. In these gardens, people raise carrots, tomatoes, beans, beets, and the like.

Most islands produce chickens, pigs, cattle, and goats. Horses can be seen here and there, but they fare best where the climate isn't too hot and humid. Nevertheless, you see many horses in Tonga, where they serve for transport and for farm work. Since lands in Oceania are seldom fenced, horses and cows will often be tied to a tree or a stake. If the rope is short, an animal may be tied by a hind leg so it can reach farther for grass. Sheep suffer in much of Oceania, especially on the low islands, where their heavy coats keep them too warm. They can be found mainly in mountainous regions, such as on New Caledonia.

The Coconut — Major Crop of Oceania

Tongans and most other islanders depend heavily on their coconut crops for earning cash. After saving enough nuts for their own use, the islanders sell the rest to be turned into copra. At a copra plant, workers chop the nuts in two and let the halves lie meat-side up on a drying platform. Too much rain during the drying process will cause the meat to mildew, and then it is good only for pig food. Otherwise, once the water content evaporates from the meat, the workers scoop it from the shell with a curved knife.

The dried meat, known as copra, contains oil, which evaporates much more slowly than the water it contains. This oil can be squeezed out. In the past, most copra traveled to France, Australia, and other foreign countries to be processed. Today, the governments of Oceania seek to have the oil produced locally. The final products—cooking oil, margarine, soap, cosmetics, and explosives—may also be manufactured in the islands someday.

Coconut trees start bearing in five to eight years. They reach their peak of production in about twenty-five years and continue to produce well for another four decades. Where people plant the palms, they stand in neat rows, but trees that take root by themselves form helter-skelter patches. Planned groves generally produce better than the haphazard ones.

Because of a lack of planning, most regions witness changes in coconut production. For instance, Tonga once sold about 20,000 tons of copra a year, but in the 1960's production dwindled to less than 10,000 tons annually. Of course, part of the reason was more people to be fed, leaving fewer nuts to be turned into copra. However, agricultural experts believe production can be increased to 65,000 tons a year. As a result, the Tongan government has begun a program of agricultural education.

Among other things, it calls for the people to grow other crops among the coconut palms. They are to plant tall crops, such as bananas and manioc, at least nine feet from the coconut trees, and shorter plants, such as kumala and taro, six feet away. Farmers are also supposed to weed among their trees at least twice a year, and to place around the trunk of each tree, ten to twenty feet above the ground, a metal band from eight inches to a foot wide. The purpose of the band is to keep rats and coconut crabs from reaching the nuts.

Fighting the Man in the Middle

Copra increases won't necessarily solve the economic problems of any island country. Prices can fluctuate greatly, and as more copra becomes available, its value may decline. In the twentieth century, the price has been as low as $10 and as high as $200 a ton, with the usual range being between $40 and $120. Individuals as well as nations suffer when prices go down.

To help themselves fare better, islanders in the Gilbert and Ellice Islands and parts of Micronesia's trust territory have started cooperative societies and stores. The men who formed these cooperatives have stopped selling copra to shippers, who had been making a good profit, and have started selling directly to foreign buyers, which has increased profits for the local people.

In Melanesia, the people have begun to see the need to work together to eliminate unfair practices. In July and August of 1970, New Caledonian farmers began to object about the importing of foodstuffs from abroad. They said the foreign produce made it nearly impossible for them to sell their own vegetables. The New Caledonians had already formed a farmers' union, but it hadn't worked well because of internal disagreements. Now, in an effort to back their complaints, they began cooperating to halt food imports.

The Sugarcane Industry

Growing sugarcane has become a major industry on many islands and has been especially profitable for Fiji. The main producer there has been the Colonial Sugar Refining Company, with headquarters in Australia. By 1970, about one out of every four people in the Fiji Islands earned most of his livelihood by serving this company, and the government received nearly a fifth of its income from sugar exports. It came as a great shock to everyone when the company announced it would withdraw from the islands sometime in 1972.

The government has talked of nationalizing the sugar industry, but it would need a great deal of financial help to manage that. In addition, any organization or group taking over the company's operations would need an agreement with some foreign power that it would buy Fijian sugar at a stable price. Great Britain was the logical country to do it, but as a member of the European Common Market, she would no longer be free to honor an agreement with Fiji. All her trade arrangements would be influenced by her membership in the Common Market.

That, in fact, was one of the main reasons why the Colonial Sugar Refining Company decided to withdraw from Fiji. Since it had been selling much of its sugar to Britain, it feared Britain's entry into the

Common Market might affect sales and prices. Another major factor bringing about the company's decision was labor unrest in the cane fields. As the company gave in to requests for better wages, it found its profits slipping.

Labor Conditions in the Pacific

Throughout Oceania, laborers generally need better wage scales. Fijian miners in the gold and manganese fields receive something like fifty cents an hour. Other Fijians make twenty-five to thirty-five cents an hour.

Young Fijians, feeling crowded out of their own country by the East Indians, sometimes go to Tonga to seek employment. Wages in Tonga average only two to three dollars a week, and the country is not in need of outsiders to fill any jobs. Observers fear this influx of foreigners will cause friction one day, as Tongans never encourage anyone to come to their islands on any basis but as tourists.

In Polynesia, Tahiti usually offers the best-paying jobs. Laborers there earn about sixty-five cents an hour for an eight-hour day and a five- or six-day week. Office workers start at about a dollar an hour and can work up to $2.50 in a dozen years or so, but then they've reached the top for their type of work. Mechanics and other workers with special training get $2.50 to $3.00 an hour.

Conditions in Micronesia may be a little better, but not necessarily. Workers serving the United States receive a dollar or more an hour. As a result, in areas where American influence is strongest, local shop-keepers and other businessmen have been forced to raise wages above fifty cents. Where American influence is weakest in Micronesia, salaries continue to be even lower.

New Zealand had labor shortages in 1970 and acquired workers from Fiji and Tonga. Island laborers went to the Hutt River Valley, northeast of Wellington, to work on farms and in industrial plants. At the end of six months, ranchers and industrialists who had used the workers returned them safely to Tonga and Fiji. New groups were then brought in to replace them until the labor shortage ended. The transportation costs and housing were taken care of by the New Zealand firms benefiting.

Mining

Many governments of Oceania hope their financial problems will be solved by the discovery of valuable minerals on their islands. Prospecting goes on somewhere in Oceania every year, but results frequently prove disappointing. Gold, found on Viti Levu in 1932, does aid the Fijian economy, and workable deposits came to light in 1955 in the Solomons. Besides having gold, New Caledonia produces large quantities of nickel and has some chromium, iron, cobalt, silver, zinc, platinum, copper, cinnabar, mercury, and coal. Some other islands also have traces of these metals, but in many cases the veins must be worked by very cheap labor for any profit to result.

Money could be made on cobalt when South Pacific sources seemed to be the major ones of the world. Important discoveries in Canada and Africa after World War II caused the prices to drop, however.

Nickel is refined in New Caledonia.

Even if prices had remained high, the cobalt producers of Oceania would have suffered. The region is poorly located to compete in world trade, because it lies far from most industrial countries except Australia, New Zealand, and Japan. Most industrialists wanting cobalt found it easier to get shipments from North America or Africa rather than all the way from New Caledonia.

In the early 1970's, a big effort to discover oil got under way in the Pacific. The Solomons, New Caledonia, and other islands of that area showed possibilities of producing petroleum, and exploratory work commenced in Fiji and Tonga. It was the first time Tongans had showed a willingness to lease large areas of land. In August 1970, the country allowed an international business group of six companies to start research. Scientists say it will take two to ten years to find out whether worthwhile quantities of petroleum exist in various parts of Oceania.

Other Industries in Oceania

Both fishing for tuna and canning it grew in importance in Micronesia during the 1960's, but since then, alarm over the content of mercury in certain seafoods has caused concern. Nevertheless, in American Samoa, industrialists made plans in 1970 to start a fish-canning business there.

Pearl divers work in the waters of the Marquesas, Tuamotus, Gambiers, Fijis, Guam, and some other islands. They also collect the shellfish from which pearl shell, or mother-of-pearl, can be obtained. Fishermen sell shark fins and bêche-de-mer, or sea slugs, to the Chinese, who use them for food.

Trees from the forests of the Pacific can sometimes be harvested profitably. The Solomons export mahogany and sandalwood, as do Guam, the Marianas, and various other islands. Teak, ebony, and ironwood also grow in Oceania. Little effort was made in the past to plant trees for the future, so some islands now lack timber for export. Unfortunately, little replanting is being done even now.

There are other problems, too. Numerous islands that possess good stands of trees lack the transportation facilities to make harvesting worth while. Getting valuable wood to a seaport for shipment presents major difficulties. Where rivers exist, of course, logs can be floated to the coast. Otherwise, logging requires roads, and many islands have almost none. Trucks large enough to handle timber would get stuck in mud much of the time.

Transportation

Highways lead to major tourist attractions or business establishments. Away from the cities they usually turn into dirt roads. Cars can be found mainly in the capitals of Oceania. Little models prove particularly popular, as well as practical, on the old, winding streets of most cities. Motorbikes and scooters can be seen frequently in the French territories, especially Tahiti, but ordinary bicycles are more numerous in British areas. All vehicles are kept operating much longer than in the United States.

Most major cities have small buses, running usually on irregular schedules. Whenever enough passengers get on to make a trip profitable, the driver starts. In more backward regions, old trucks serve as buses, with boards across the back for seats. The newest buses generally belong to hotels, especially those built away from the heart of town. They provide the hotel guests with service to the downtown area. Everywhere, increasing numbers of buses, cars, and other vehicles create traffic problems. It can be a major ordeal to get past a market early in the morning when farmers are arriving with carts or small trucks filled with produce.

Usually, good roads connect major cities with airports. Since the cities of Oceania grew up around harbors, they may be miles from areas suitable for landing fields. Jets cannot land at Suva, but must go to Nandi on the far side of Fiji's main island. Anyone going to the capital from Nandi must rent a car to drive around the edge of the island or must transfer to a small plane. Until 1971, shuttle flights from Nandi to Suva operated only during daylight hours, but night flights began after the capital's airport had been sufficiently lighted and modernized to receive them.

Fiji Airways has ordered one jet plane of its own from Britain. If it earns a profit, they will obtain others. In addition to flights between Nandi and Suva, Fiji Airways serves other islands of the country and also flies to Tonga.

The traveler can reach American Samoa by jet, after which he has a long ride on a winding road to get into Pago Pago. Before the air age reached Tahiti, the coastal land suitable for landing strips had already been taken up by settlements, hotels, industrial plants, and private homes. As a result, engineers built Papeete's landing field on a coral reef. Travel agents say modern tourism in Oceania started with the opening of Papeete's airstrip in 1960.

The Profitable Trade of Tourism

Before jet planes, most visitors to the Pacific arrived on a cruise ship or a freighter. Although some spent time ashore, many people lived on the vessels and set foot on land only long enough to see a few sights and buy some souvenirs.

The traveler who really wants to learn something about Oceania stays in a small local hotel. He drives, for cars can be rented in capital cities, or walks wherever possible. However, the Pacific is one region of the world where it becomes almost essential for the visitor to take some guided tours. Otherwise he needs an unlimited amount of time to spend in getting to out-of-the-way places. Many of the prearranged tours are definitely worth their cost.

Tourism has become one of the outstanding industries of Oceania. Tahiti, the Samoas, Tonga, and Fiji in particular depend on it to bring money from outside. Early in the 1960's, these islands felt they had a good year if they saw 10,000 to 20,000 visitors, but with giant 747 planes coming to the South Pacific since 1971, 150,000 to 200,000 tourists can be expected annually.

Nobody knows how all these people will find places to sleep or eat, but hotel construction should boom in Oceania during the 1970's. Six tourist hotels, to be constructed in Micronesia, appeared to be just a beginning. Yapese leaders objected that one of the new hotels was to be built there, for they feared that large numbers of tourists would affect their way of life. They also suspected that their people would not be the ones to benefit from the tourists—that, while outsiders reaped the profits, the local people would probably end up holding doors, waiting on tables, mopping out rest rooms, opening packing crates, and being searched for stolen goods.

Many visitors to Oceania will find satisfaction; others will be disappointed. Tourists will probably feel most welcome in British and former British areas and least welcome in French territories, although it won't be the local people who will make them feel unwelcome. If they stay in small hotels, they may feel as though they belong to a family, but at the luxury places they could get the impression that only their money matters. Tahiti in particular has extremely high prices, which showed no signs of declining in the early 1970's. A cup of tea was fifty cents or more, and a hamburger, if you could find a place to order one, cost well over a dollar.

Most large hotels have a section of beach. On the windward side of an island, beaches become cluttered with debris, washed and blown ashore, but hotels have attendants to clear it away. In addition to a beach, a hotel generally has a pool. Local children and even some young adults often slip through fences and use these hotel pools until someone chases them away.

Sights for Tourists to See

Many people go to the islands simply to relax at the hotels and in the pools. But attractions await people who want to sightsee. Pago Pago has an aerial tramway connecting peaks on opposite sides of the harbor. From this you can look down on one of the most gorgeous settings of the Pacific. A visit to the heart of town proves disappointing, however, for it has a seedy appearance on close inspection.

Tourism is the fastest-growing industry of the Pacific islands.

Realizing its island of Vavau offered more attractive scenery than Tongatapu, Tonga ordered a ferry from England to take tourists between the two islands. It arrived in 1971 and offered sailings three times a week. Britain, of course, helped finance the ferry.

Fiji provides two unusual treats—firewalking and turtle calling. The firewalkers of Mbengga, or Bequa, Island belong to the Sawau tribe. They fill a pit twelve feet square by five feet deep with rocks, and then burn logs on them for twenty-four hours. Only the men of one family group do the walking, and they claim to talk with a spirit before they undertake the feat. When the spirit assures them of its aid, they come from the hut in which they have remained concealed and walk barefoot across the red-hot stones without being burned.

Various explanations for their ability to cross the pit have been offered. One is that the men have toughened their feet by a lifetime of going barefoot. Probably as boys they started practicing on warm

204

coals and gradually worked up to hotter ones until they could stand more heat than most men.

The latest scientific theory is that the rocks used absorb heat easily and glow at much lower temperatures than most rocks. The burning wood turns the rocks red without making them fiery hot. When a man is burned, which has happened, the firewalkers say he has broken one of the taboos connected with the ritual. But it is possible he has accidentally stepped on a bit of firewood that wasn't raked away.

Turtle callers live on Kandavru Island, also in Fiji. Women from the village of Namuana go to rocks above a bay and chant a song of ancient times. After a while, as if in response, a turtle rises to the surface of the bay. Of course, turtles have to come to the surface to breathe, so maybe the women sit and sing until a turtle comes up. Yet it is reported that if men from a certain village are present, no turtles will show themselves. The huge reptiles still have to breathe, so why would they surface in sight at one time and out of sight at another? A satisfactory answer remains to be found. In other parts of Oceania, certain tribesmen reportedly call sharks, eels, or prawns.

Micronesia's ancient ruins, Nanmatol, at Ponape would be a tourist attraction if they could be reached easily. The walls of the old capital consist of great rocks, carved into log shapes by some long-forgotten process. Scientists puzzle over how a primitive people could have moved the huge blocks of basalt, a volcanic rock. Radiocarbon dating shows that the area was occupied as recently as 1200, but the original inhabitants may have been there centuries earlier. Perhaps the stonework has some relation to the great carvings of heads at Easter Island, which are better known because of their accessibility. The ruins of Ponape are scattered about dozens of tiny islets and for the most part can be visited easily only during high tide.

If the tourist industry grows in Oceania as rapidly as predicted, travel agents will try to get visitors to these and other unusual sights. No doubt the tourists will bring many changes so that the Oceania of the future will be different from the Oceania of today.

A New Direction

Once a region of warring tribes, Oceania became an area of colonies after Europeans discovered it. Now the trend sees it developing into independent nations. If the leaders of the islands are wise, they will go a step farther and cooperate with one another instead of trying to survive as competitors. A United States of Oceania seems unlikely, but many observers feel a swing in that direction is desirable.

The South Pacific Commission

A step along the way came in 1948 with the formation of the South Pacific Commission. Created with United Nations assistance to aid Melanesia primarily, it nevertheless studied and recommended "measures for the welfare and advancement of South Sea Islanders." Now it serves Polynesia and Micronesia as well.

The people of the Pacific are beginning to demand better jobs and the return of their land where they have lost control of it. Although the British progress toward giving their islands independence, the French are far behind them, and the United States military has a firm grip on Micronesia. If American bases are necessary for international security—and perhaps they are—they should at least be maintained with the consent of independent Micronesians.

No commission can accomplish everything, of course. Each nation and each group of islands must be willing to work harder toward settling the internal problems of the Pacific.

Motor bikes and scooters mingle with small cars in the heart of Papeete, Tahiti.

This Fijian, in his prime, is considered young by the elders who control life in his village.

Overcoming prejudice is one field in which all the people of Oceania could improve, but they might do so faster if the leading nations of the world, such as the United States, Britain, Russia, and France, were to set a better example for them to follow. For instance, Fiji's political temperature is sure to affect that country's rate of advancement as well as that of the whole South Pacific. If the East Indians and Fijians ever come to blows, tourists might be frightened away by the unrest. All the same, with the East Indians increasing in numbers almost twice as fast as the Fijians, it will take intelligent effort on everybody's part to avoid open clashes.

The Generation Gap

Another trouble area in the Pacific involves the generation gap. It isn't a matter of teen-agers objecting to the ways and thinking of their parents, but of most people living under the control of elderly chiefs

208

and family heads. Almost none of these senior citizens have much, if any, education, yet they ignore younger men who are getting high school or college training. Inevitably, changes must occur in this old system.

The Enemy — the Crown of Thorns

Even nature must give in to alterations. If it doesn't, scientists fear parts of the South Pacific will cease to exist. This is true where atolls and islands remain above the ocean's surface because they have the protection of living coral reefs. In the 1960's, those reefs came under attack from a spiny starfish known as the crown of thorns.

As far as anyone knows, the main food of the starfish has always been the coral polyp. Yet in the past the polyps managed to build great colonies stretching tens to hundreds of miles in length. Lying just below the surface of the water—or just above, if raised by earth movements—these coral colonies have limited the action of waves. They have left quiet areas in which fish thrive, and often they have protected atolls or islands from being pounded to pieces by breakers.

Early in the 1960's, the starfish began to multiply at an unusual rate. They spread throughout the Pacific wherever waters are warm enough to provide habitats for coral. Instead of eating just at night, they started devouring the polyps twenty-four hours a day.

The crown of thorns has a central disk, or body, from which twelve to eighteen spine-covered arms extend. A large one will have a body a foot in diameter, with tentacles reaching out another six inches beyond that. In a day's time, one crown of thorns can eat an area of polyps about two feet square. Although that hardly sounds alarming, "packs" of starfish working on a coral reef can kill a stretch a mile long in a few months. With the live coral gone, the reef has no protective cover. Sea worms bore into dead coral and weaken it, and storm-driven waves batter it until it crumbles away. In a little over two years, twenty miles of Guam's coast have almost been wiped out in this way. If the crown of thorns isn't soon brought under control, islands and atolls protected by coral reefs may disappear completely before the erosive crashing of the waves.

Local divers seek out these killer starfish, impale them on spears, and bury them on shore, so that they are sure to die. Spearing them and leaving them in the water guarantees nothing, for the hardy starfish mend their wounds and go on destroying polyps. If cut in two, a crown of thorns frequently becomes two enemies instead of one, for both halves may live. It takes time to locate the killers, spear them, and drag them ashore. As a result, islanders who are busy supporting families can't fight much of a war against the starfish. They must have help from modern science, and they began receiving it late in the 1960's.

Scuba divers inject formaldehyde into the crown of thorns to kill it. A scuba diver can shoot lethal doses into 150 starfish in an area the size of a football field before he runs low on air. He must, of course, avoid the thornlike barbs sticking out from the arms and body. Their poison can make a man sick, although it won't kill him.

The crown of thorns is a threat to living coral.

Scientists also seek to fight the starfish with its natural enemies. The giant triton, a large snail in a sturdy spiral shell that protects it from the poisonous spines of the crown of thorns, is one of the few marine animals that eats the killer. Scientists at Australia's University of Queensland hope to raise tritons and distribute them where crown of thorns do the most damage.

Researchers also hope to learn why the starfish have suddenly gotten out of control. Man himself is probably to blame. A female crown of thorns lays millions of eggs in her lifetime, but few of them survive. Fish and other marine creatures eat some eggs, and after the tiny larvae hatch out they, too, are eaten. But where man takes or drives away sea animals, he gives the eggs and the larvae a chance to thrive. Collectors pay good sums for the lovely giant triton shells, so divers have reduced their numbers by cashing in on the demand for them.

Engineering projects may also be at fault. Where men dredge and blast to improve channels and harbors, they drive away many sea animals. Perhaps starfish feel the effects of changes less than their enemies do and remain. Possibly nuclear blasts have killed the enemies of starfish without affecting the crown of thorns themselves. It has even been suggested that insect sprays, used on land to get rid of mosquitoes, have washed into the sea and killed the enemies but not the starfish. With fewer natural enemies, the crown of thorns have increased rapidly.

Typhoons

To improve living conditions in Oceania, man must battle nature above the ocean's surface. Typhoons take lives and destroy property every year. Although the prevention of bad storms may be impossible, scientists are taking steps to cut down on the amount of destruction they cause.

The United States Air Force operates a typhoon-alert station on Guam, which warns the entire Marianas region of approaching storms. Whereas heavy winds once took dozens to hundreds of lives in that area, some recent storms have taken no lives at all. Guam's worst typhoon in

Nukualofa's new post office has been built to withstand storms.

recorded history, in 1962, killed only nine people. Yet its winds of over 225 miles an hour did more damage to buildings and crops than the destructive fighting of World War II. Similar warning systems need to be set up throughout Oceania.

Cooperation makes a warning system, a fight against starfish, or any other effort at improvement work. When outsiders and local people all accept this fact, Oceania will advance into modern times. It is hoped that this change can come about without causing the beautiful South Pacific to lose its fascinating heritage from the past.

Historical Highlights

3000–2000   Southeast Asians probably settle on some Melanesian islands.
2500–1500   Asians probably settle in Micronesia.
2000   Pacific islanders begin to change from being food gatherers and hunters to being farmers.
1000–500   Some peoples of Oceania probably start permanent settlements in Polynesia.

800–1200   The great migrations across the Pacific probably taper off, with most livable islands being occupied.
1513   Vasco Nuñez de Balboa "discovers" the Pacific Ocean.
1521   Ferdinand Magellan and his seamen reach Guam and become the first Europeans known to see an island of Oceania.
1526 or 1527 Diego da Rocha visits several islands of Oceania, probably in the western Carolines.
1528   Alvaro de Saavedra discovers the eastern Carolines.
1529   Spain and Portugal reach an agreement that gives Oceania to Spain.
1543   Ruy López de Villalobos discovers the Palau Islands.
1568   Álvaro de Mendaña de Neyra discovers the Solomon Islands.
1579   Francis Drake, sailing around the world and raiding Spanish treasure ships, passes through Oceania.
1595   Mendaña discovers the Marquesas and the Santa Cruz Islands.
1605–1606   Pedro Fernandes de Queirós discovers islands in the Tuamotu Archipelago, the Society Islands, and the New Hebrides.
1616   Willem Schouten and Jacob Le Maire reach the Pacific, where they discover several islands.
1639–1644   Abel Tasman makes voyages of discovery in the Pacific.
1667   Jesuit missionaries leave Spain to Christianize Pacific islanders.
1686   Francisco Lazeano takes possession of the Carolines for Spain and names them for its king, Carlos II.

1722	Jakob Roggeveen discovers Easter Island and part of the Samoas.
1740–1744	George Anson leads a British expedition to attack Spanish shipping in Oceania.
1765	John Byron crosses the Pacific on the first purely scientific voyage through Oceania.
1767	Samuel Wallis discovers Tahiti, the Wallis Islands, and others.
1768	Louis Antoine de Bougainville claims the Society Islands for France and discovers the island in the Solomons that now bears his name.
1768–1771	James Cook makes his first Pacific voyage of exploration and discovery.
1772–1775	Cook makes his second great voyage.
1776	A British whaling vessel is perhaps the first to operate in Oceania's waters.
1776–1779	Cook makes his last voyage to Oceania and is killed in Hawaii.
1785–1788	The Comte de La Pérouse heads a scientific expedition to Oceania.
1788–1789	William Bligh takes the *Bounty* to Tahiti to collect breadfruit seedlings and causes one of history's most famous mutinies.
1790	American, British, and French whalers turn the Pacific into a major fishing ground.
1797	Protestant missionaries reach Oceania and seek converts in Tahiti.
1841	Herman Melville starts a voyage to Oceania that provides material for some of his most famous books.
1842	France takes control of the Marquesas.
1843	Catholic missionaries arrive in New Caledonia.
1845	Tonga's current royal family comes to power.
1847	Islanders that may have been the first blackbirds are taken from the New Hebrides and put to work in Australia.
1850–1860	Whaling in the Pacific reaches its peak.
1853	France occupies New Caledonia.
1856	The United States' Guano Act allows Americans to claim uninhabited islands of Oceania in order to mine guano deposits.
1864	France begins using New Caledonia as a penal colony.
1872	A British Kidnaping Act gives naval officers authority to capture blackbirders and take them to Australia for trial; sugar production in Fiji starts what will become a major industry; the

	United States sets up a coaling station at Pago Pago in the Samoas.
1874	Fiji becomes a British protectorate.
1875	Spain tries to control all trade in Micronesia, an impossible undertaking.
1880	France annexes the Tubuai Islands.
1884	Germany annexes the Bismarck Archipelago, and the following year takes over the Marshalls.
1887	France and Britain agree on joint control of the New Hebrides.
1888	Britain annexes the Cook Islands, but gives them to New Zealand in 1890.
1889	Robert Louis Stevenson settles in western Samoa.
1891	Paul Gauguin goes to Tahiti to paint.
1892	Britain establishes a protectorate over the Gilbert and Ellice islands.
1898	United States military forces take control of Guam during the Spanish-American War; Germany starts to replace Spain as a major power in Oceania.
1899	Spain sells the Carolines to Germany; Germany establishes control over western Samoa.
1900	The United States annexes American Samoa.
1901	Tonga becomes a British protectorate; New Zealand claims Niue Island.
1902	Queensland becomes the last region of Australia to outlaw blackbirding.
1914–1918	Japan replaces Germany as a major power in Micronesia during World War I.
1920	The Marianas, Carolines, and Marshalls are mandated to Japan by the League of Nations.
1921	Japan, the United States, Britain, and France agree not to fortify or use as bases the islands of Oceania.
1932	Gold is discovered in the Fiji Islands.
1936	Japan refuses to renew agreements against fortifying Oceanic islands or using them as bases.
1937	Amelia Earhart disappears in Oceania.
1940	Passenger planes begin making regular stops at Fiji and New Caledonia.
1941	Japan launches a program of military conquest in the Pacific.

1942	Japanese advances in Oceania are halted and the Allies start to recover lost islands.
1944	Major battles in Oceania end as World War II moves closer to the Japanese heartland.
1946	The first of twenty-three nuclear tests takes place at Bikini Island.
1947	The United Nations gives the United States the responsibility for overseeing the Trust Territory of the Pacific Islands.
1948	The South Pacific Commission is formed to help South Sea Islanders advance into modern times.
1955	Gold is discovered in the Solomon Islands.
1962	Western Samoa becomes independent; the Cook Islands turn down independence.
1963	English becomes the language of instruction in all schools of the United States Trust Territory of the Pacific Islands.
1965	The congress of Micronesia holds its first meeting.
1967	Tahiti begins television broadcasts.
1968	Nauru Island achieves independence; the University of the South Pacific opens in Fiji.
1969	The territorial assembly of French Polynesia votes for more self-government, but fails to get it.
1970	Bikini is officially returned to its people; Micronesian officials reject a United States proposal to give the area commonwealth status and demand full independence; American Samoa elects a delegate-at-large to the United States Congress; Fiji and Tonga achieve independence; Pitcairn Island receives a coat of arms.
1971	Tonga opens a modern hospital; giant jet passenger planes start serving the South Pacific.

Other Books of Interest

The books starred were written especially with young readers in mind.

Attenborough, David, *People of Paradise*. New York: Harper & Row, 1960.

Belshaw, Cyril S., *Changing Melanesia*. Melbourne, Australia: Oxford University Press, 1954.

Borden, Charles A., *South Sea Islands*. Philadelphia: Macrae Smith Co., 1961.

Burdick, Eugene, *The Blue of Capricorn*. Boston: Houghton Mifflin Co., 1961.

* Caldwell, John C., *Let's Visit the South Pacific*. New York: John Day Co., 1963.

* Cavanna, Betty, *The First Book of Fiji*. New York: Franklin Watts Inc., 1969.

Cumberland, Kenneth B., *Southwest Pacific*. New York: McGraw-Hill Book Co., 1956.

Fornander, Abraham, *An Account of the Polynesian Race: Its Origins and Migrations*. Rutland, Vt.: Charles E. Tuttle Co., 1969.

* Geis, Darlene, ed., *Let's Travel in the South Seas*. Chicago: Childrens Press, 1965.

* Harrington, Lyn, *Australia and New Zealand: Pacific Community*. Camden, N.J.: Thomas Nelson Inc., 1969.

Kahn, E. J., Jr., *A Reporter in Micronesia*. New York: W. W. Norton & Co., 1966.

Michener, James A., *Return to Paradise*. New York: Random House, 1951.

Moorhead, Alan, *The Fatal Impact*. New York: Harper & Row, 1966.

* Newton, Douglas, *Seafarers of the Pacific*. Cleveland, Ohio: World Publishing Co., 1964.

Oliver, Douglas L., *The Pacific Islands*. Garden City, N.Y.: Doubleday & Co., 1961.

Phelan, Nancy, *Atoll Holiday*. Sydney, Australia: Angus & Robertson Ltd., 1958.

* Quinn, Vernon, *Picture Map Geography of the Pacific Islands*. Philadelphia: J. B. Lippincott Co., 1964.

* Rose, Ronald, *Inoke Sails the South Seas*. New York: Harcourt, Brace & World, 1966.

Russell, Alexander, *Aristocrats of the South Seas*. New York: Roy Publishers, 1961.

Shadbolt, Maurice, and Ruhen, Olaf, *Isles of the South Pacific*. Washington, D.C.: National Geographic Society, 1968.

Suggs, Robert C., *The Hidden Worlds of Polynesia*. New York: Harcourt, Brace & World, 1962.

* Suggs, Robert C., *Lords of the Blue Pacific*. Greenwich, Conn.: New York Graphic Society, 1962.

Villiers, Alan, *The Coral Sea*. New York: McGraw-Hill Book Co., 1949.

Watters, R. F., *Koro*. London: Oxford University Press, 1969.

Williams, Maslyn, *The Stone Age Island*. Garden City, N.Y.: Doubleday & Co., 1964.

Index

World Neighbors

Written to introduce the reader to his contemporaries in other lands and to sketch the background needed for an understanding of the world today, these books are well-documented, revealing presentations. Based on firsthand knowledge of the country and illustrated with unusual photographs, the text is informal and inviting. Geographical, historical, and cultural data are woven unobtrusively into accounts of daily life. Maps, working index, chronology, and bibliography are useful additions.